Fee Fi Fo Fum

Puppets & Other Folktale Fun

Linda Bair & Jill Andrews

Fort Atkinson, Wisconsin

To our moms—
their creativity and positive natures are always an inspiration.

Published by UpstartBooks
W5527 State Rd. 106
P.O. Box 800
Fort Atkinson, Wisconsin 53538-0800
1-800-448-4887

© 2005 Linda Bair and Jill Andrews.
Cover design: Debra Neu

The paper used in this publication meets the minimum requirements of American National Standard
for Information Science — Permanence of Paper for Printed Library Material. ANSI/NISO Z39.48-1992.

Table of Contents

Introduction

Fee Fi Fo Fum is designed as a resource for the media center and primary classroom (kindergarten through second grade), but public libraries and preschools will find that they can easily adapt the literature and activities to meet their specific programming needs.

This book is divided into three sections: Animals, People and Places. Each section contains 10 folktales, which are the basis for a set of activities. The activities feature the folktale as well as a puppet activity, a list of selected children's books, crafts and art ideas, games and curriculum tie-ins.

The stories and activities can and should be adapted in any way that fits your programming needs. Bibliography books can be replaced with your favorites or a title available in your library. While all books were chosen because of their wide availability in school and public libraries, many titles go out of print very quickly and may not be available for purchase.

Preparation times are not given, but all activities were chosen with the ease of preparation in mind. The puppet activities generally require the most time to prepare. Most of the activities take a maximum of 15 minutes to complete, but some of the puppet and craft activities will require more time.

Using Puppets in Programming

Puppets are found in many cultures. They can bring stories more alive for children as they help reinforce verbal skills. Gardner's theory of multiple intelligences lists the following intelligences: verbal/linguistic, logical/mathematical, visual/spatial, body/kinesthetic, musical/rhythmic, interpersonal, intrapersonal and naturalistic. Making and using puppets can incorporate all of the intelligences.

The puppets in this book are designed to be used at actual size unless otherwise indicated. Use heavier paper, such as card stock, whenever possible. Even after completing a puppet activity in the book, read the story often and encourage the children to use the puppets individually, to play with them in small groups (perhaps with a reader/narrator/listening station and puppeteers), to tell the story to others and to invent new stories for the characters.

Puppets are fun and highly motivational. Encourage the children to create their own puppets for other stories or for other subjects such as science or social studies. Keep the following supplies on hand if possible.

- card stock
- construction paper
- crayons
- markers
- scissors
- paper bags (lunch size and grocery size)
- popsicle sticks
- paper plates
- paint sticks
- Styrofoam cups
- glue, paste or glue sticks
- fabric scraps
- buttons
- yarn
- pipe cleaners
- dried lima beans or pasta shells

Animals

Anansi

Programming Ideas

Theme: Spiders

Setting the Scene

Ask if any of the children have ever heard of Anansi. Can they tell the class what kind of an animal he is? *(Spider.)* Explain that Anansi is the main character in many African and Jamaican folktales. Sometimes Anansi is human, a kind of "spider man," but usually Anansi is a spider.

Story

Anansi and the Moss-Covered Rock
by Eric A. Kimmel

After reading the story, discuss how the deer did not follow the language pattern that the other animals did and how he was able to trick Anansi. Explain that many jokes follow patterns, especially "Knock-Knock" jokes. Share some jokes with the class and ask them to share jokes they know.

Puppets

Make Anansi puppets (page 11). Have the children dramatize the story as you read it, with the children acting out the parts (except for the puppeteer using an Anansi puppet). Dramatize the story again with the children making up their own dialogue. Children can perform the story at home or at a center using stuffed animals.

Activities

Art

Read *The Magic Weaver of Rugs* or Osborne's retelling of the Arachne myth in "The Weaving Contest." Discuss how important weaving has been to people in the past. Make place mats (page 66).

Folklore

Read other Anansi tales. Discuss how stories sometimes give animals attributes they do not really have.

Game

Discuss how the little bush deer is hidden in some of the illustrations. Name other animals that blend into their surroundings. Read *What Color Is Camouflage?* to learn more about animal camouflage. Make several large chameleons or spiders (page 12) in different colors that match items in the classroom. Hide one or more of them and have the children look around to find them. Put some hidden picture books such as *They Thought They Saw Him, Animalia* or *Have You Seen My Duckling?* at a reading center.

Research and Reading

Read books like *Spiders* or *Spider's Lunch* to learn more about spiders. Read *Be Nice to Spiders, How Spider Stopped the Litterbugs* or *The Lady and the Spider* for fun.

Rock Collecting

Ask children to bring interesting rocks to show the class. Try to identify them. Invite a guest speaker if possible. Read *Sylvester and the Magic Pebble* for fun.

Science

Read McDermott's version of *Anansi the Spider* or *The Five Chinese Brothers* by Claire Bishop. Discuss the concept that offspring are very much like their parents and each other, but not exactly. Learn more about animal babies in books like *Baby Animals* or *Amazing Animal Babies.*

Books

Folktale Versions

Arkhurst, Joyce Cooper. *The Adventures of Spider—West African Folk Tales.* Little, Brown and Company, 1964. Six Anansi tales.

Cole, Joanna (ed). *Best-Loved Folktales of the World.* Doubleday, 1982. A collection of 200 folktales from around the world.

Haley, Gail E. *A Story, A Story.* Macmillan, 1970. Anansi, the Spider man, buys the Sky God's stories and brings them to Earth.

Kimmel, Eric A. *Anansi and the Magic Stick.* Holiday House, 2001. Anansi takes Hyena's magic stick and the magic gets out of control.

Kimmel, Eric A. *Anansi and the Moss-Covered Rock.* Holiday House, 1988. Anansi tricks other animals with a magic rock until Little Bush Deer tricks him.

Kimmel, Eric A. *Anansi Goes Fishing.* Holiday House, 1992. Anansi tries to trick Turtle into doing all the work involved with fishing.

McDermott, Gerald. *Anansi the Spider: A Tale From the Ashanti.* Henry Holt & Company, 1972. Anansi's six sons rescue him.

Temple, Frances. *Tiger Soup: An Anansi Story From Jamaica.* Richard Jackson Books, 1994. Anansi eats Tiger's soup and manages to put the blame on the monkeys.

Related Reading

Bailey, Donna. *Spiders.* Steck-Vaughn, 1991. Photographs and text describe different spiders and their characteristics.

Base, Graeme. *Animalia.* H. N. Abrams, 1986. An alphabet book featuring animals with a picture of the author as a boy hidden in each illustration.

Bishop, Claire Huchet. *The Five Chinese Brothers.* Putnam, 1996. The classic children's book, first published in 1938, of how five brothers save each other because of their amazing abilities.

Brown, Andrew. *Baby Animals.* Crabtree Publishing, 1997. A brief look at animals from kangaroos to frogs to whales.

Cole, Joanna. *Spider's Lunch: All About Garden Spiders.* Grosset & Dunlap, 1995. A simple look at a female garden spider.

Graham, Margaret Bloy. *Be Nice to Spiders.* HarperCollins, 1967. Helen the spider helps the zoo animals.

Kraus, Robert. *How Spider Stopped the Litterbugs.* Scholastic, 1991. Spider and his school friends turn the litterbugs into jitterbugs.

Maynard, Christopher. *Amazing Animal Babies.* Knopf, 1993. Discusses aspects of animal life such as food, playing, transportation, etc.

McNulty, Faith. *The Lady and the Spider.* Harper & Row, 1986. A spider lives in a head of lettuce in a lady's garden.

Osborne, Mary Pope. *Favorite Greek Myths.* Scholastic, 1989. Twelve Greek myths including "The Weaving Contest."

Otto, Carolyn. *What Color Is Camouflage?* HarperCollins, 1996. A look at how animals have colors, patterns or shapes that help them by fooling others' eyes.

Oughton, Jerrie. *The Magic Weaver of Rugs.* Houghton Mifflin, 1994. Spider Woman teaches two Navajo women to weave.

Steig, William. *Sylvester and the Magic Pebble.* Simon & Schuster, 1980. Sylvester finds a magic pebble, which grants wishes when held.

Strete, Craig Kee. *They Thought They Saw Him.* Greenwillow Books, 1996. A chameleon finds safety from different predators by changing colors.

Tafuri, Nancy. *Have You Seen My Duckling?* Scholastic, 1984. A mother duck and seven ducklings look for the missing one.

Anansi: Puppet

Materials:

- black construction paper* 12" x 18"
  (1 sheet per student)
- scissors
- yarn
- tape or glue
- ruler
- pencil or light crayon

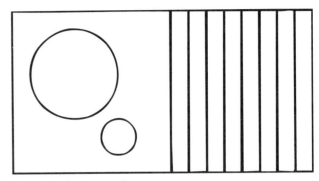

construction paper layout

Directions:

1. Use a bowl or lid from a pot approximately 8" in diameter and draw a circle. With a ruler, measure 4" to the center of the circle and make a dot. Draw a line from the center to the outside edge. This is the spider's body.

2. Draw a circle approximately 2" in diameter for the head.

3. Draw eight 1" x 12" lines for the legs.

4. Cut out all of the pieces.

5. Cut the line in the large circle to the dot.

6. Cut a piece of yarn 12" long and attach it with tape to the inside of the circle.

7. Form a cone and draw the yarn to the outside. Tape the cone underneath and on top to secure.

8. Draw eyes on the head and tape or paste the head to the cone.

9. Fold the legs into accordion pleats and attach them to the spider underneath.

* You can substitute paper plates for the spider's body if you wish. For younger children, draw the parts or make patterns for them to trace.

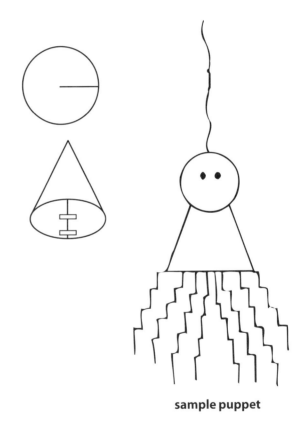

sample puppet

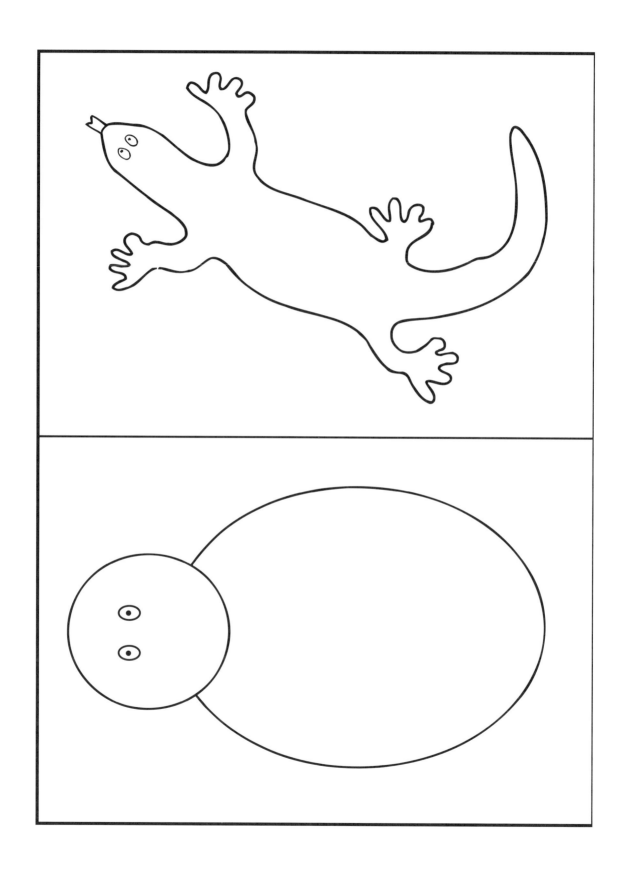

The Ant and the Grasshopper

Programming Ideas

Theme: Insects

Setting the Scene

Ask the class to name as many insects as possible. If spiders or ticks are mentioned, explain that they are arachnids with four pairs of legs instead of the three pairs of legs that insects have. Explain that the story you are about to read features two kinds of insects: ants and grasshoppers. Ask the children to tell the class anything they can about ants and grasshoppers.

Story

The Ant and the Grasshopper
by Amy Lowry Poole

After reading the story, ask the children to name the four seasons. Discuss how the illustrator/storyteller used a place she knew for the setting of the story. (Poole lived near the Summer Palace in Beijing for four years.) Ask the children to think of a setting for the story—the swing set on the playground, a flower garden at home, a tree on the way to school, etc. They should draw that setting four times, with each drawing showing a different season. If you do the puppet activity, the pictures can be the backdrops for the plays.

Puppets

Make the puppets (page 15). Have the students practice telling the story on their own. Ask for volunteers to perform for the class. Read ant and grasshopper stories like *Two Bad Ants, Effie* and *Grasshopper on the Road* and retell them using the puppets.

Activities

Character Education

Who would you like to have as a friend—the grasshopper or the ant? Why? Discuss if it is possible to work hard and have time to play. How? Is this a good thing?

Movement

Read *One Hundred Hungry Ants.* Discuss how ants move in a line. Learn the song "The Ants Go Marching" and move about in an ant parade.

Music

What is the grasshopper playing in the story? *(A violin or fiddle.)* Read other books with musical themes such as *Imani's Music, Mole Music, When Uncle Took the Fiddle* or *Little Bobo.* Ask a musician to come in and demonstrate an instrument.

Nature Journal

Go outside and look for insects. Observe how they move. Try to draw some. If possible, get an ant farm so you can more closely observe the insect world.

Research and Reading

Read books such as *It's a Good Thing There Are Insects, Bugs A to Z* or *The Best Book of Bugs* to learn more about insects. Read *Old Black Fly, The Very Hungry Caterpillar* or *The Little Squeegy Bug* for fun. Have each student pick an insect and write a story or draw a picture to share.

Science

Ask: Will you find plants or animals up high in the mountains? Deep at the bottom of the ocean? In deserts? Under rocks? Explain that living things are found almost everywhere on Earth. Ants, for instance, are just about everywhere. Read *Thinking About Ants* or *Armies of Ants.* Discuss where they live. Find out about life in the oceans and in icy regions, too.

Books

Folktale Versions

Pinkney, Jerry. *Aesop's Fables.* SeaStar Books, 2000. A collection of almost 60 stories with morals, including "The Grasshopper and the Ants."

Poole, Amy Lowry. *The Ant and the Grasshopper.* Holiday House, 2000. Ants prepare for winter outside the Imperial Chinese Emperor's summer palace, but a grasshopper does not.

Related Reading

Allinson, Beverley. *Effie.* Scholastic, 1990. Effie's loud voice saves many insects and gains her an unexpected friend.

Aylesworth, Jim. *Old Black Fly.* Henry Holt & Company, 1992. An alphabet book about an old black fly buzzing around a kitchen.

Brenner, Barbara. *Thinking About Ants.* Mondo Publishing, 1997. A brief overview of ants.

Carle, Eric. *The Very Hungry Caterpillar.* Philomel Books, 1969. A little caterpillar eats, grows big and becomes a butterfly.

DeGezelle, Terri. *Bugs A to Z.* A+ Books, 2000. Introduces a bug for every letter of the alphabet.

Fowler, Allan. *It's a Good Thing There Are Insects.* Children's Press, 1990. A brief look at insects and their part in the food chain.

Gray, Libba Moore. *When Uncle Took the Fiddle.* Orchard Books, 1999. A family wakes up and joins in after Uncle starts playing his fiddle.

Hayes, Geoffrey. *The Ants Go Marching.* HarperFestival, 1999. A lift-the-flap version of the song.

Llewellyn, Claire. *The Best Book of Bugs.* Kingfisher, 1998. A brief look at some bugs such as bees, dragonflies, beetles and spiders.

Lobel, Arnold. *Grasshopper on the Road.* HarperTrophy, 1978. Six easy-to-read stories about Grasshopper's journey.

Martin, Bill Jr., and Michael Sampson. *The Little Squeegy Bug.* Winslow Press, 2001. A little bug wants to be a bumblebee but is given a different name and purpose.

McPhail, David. *Mole Music.* Henry Holt & Company, 1999. Mole hears a beautiful violin playing on television and learns to play the violin, too.

Pinczes, Elinor J. *One Hundred Hungry Ants.* Houghton Mifflin, 1993. Ants march to a picnic but lose time when one persuades them to change formations.

Retan, Walter. *Armies of Ants.* Scholastic, 1994. An overview of ants.

Romanelli, Serena. *Little Bobo.* North-South Books, 1995. A little orangutan learns to play a violin and is sad after a crocodile eats it.

Van Allsburg, Chris. *Two Bad Ants.* Houghton Mifflin, 1988. Two ants have an adventure.

Williams, Sheron. *Imani's Music.* Atheneum Books, 2002. An African grasshopper discovers music and brings it down to Africa, then over to the Americas on a slave ship.

Ant and Grasshopper: Puppets

Materials:

- green and brown construction paper
- scissors
- glue or tape
- popsicle sticks
- pipe cleaners
- yarn
- hole punch

General Directions:

1. Photocopy the patterns on colored paper, or create patterns to be traced on construction paper.

2. Cut the pattern pieces.

Ant Directions:

1. Attach the thorax (midsection) to the rear, pasting it on the top.

2. Glue the head to the midsection. Draw on the eyes.

3. Take two pipe cleaners (per ant) and cut them in half. Take three halves and fold them in half once more to form six legs. Tape the legs to the back of the ant. Fold the bottom of each to form feet. The last half is for the antennae.

4. Punch a hole in the midsection and one in the back.

5. Cut two pieces of yarn 8 to 10 inches long. Run one through each, tying a knot at the top.

6. Run the popsicle sticks through the loops.

Grasshopper Directions:

1. Attach the three body sections.

2. Cut one pipe cleaner in half to form the legs. Attach them to the back of the grasshopper's body and bend the bottoms to form the feet.

3. Attach the wings on top of the legs.

4. Attach a popsicle stick to the back.

5. Add small pieces of pipe cleaner for the antennae.

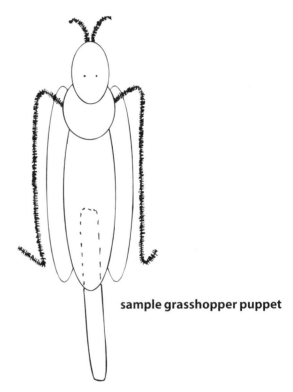

sample grasshopper puppet

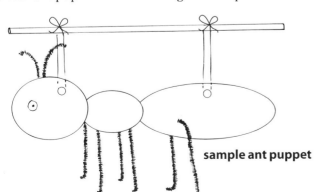

sample ant puppet

Ant Patterns

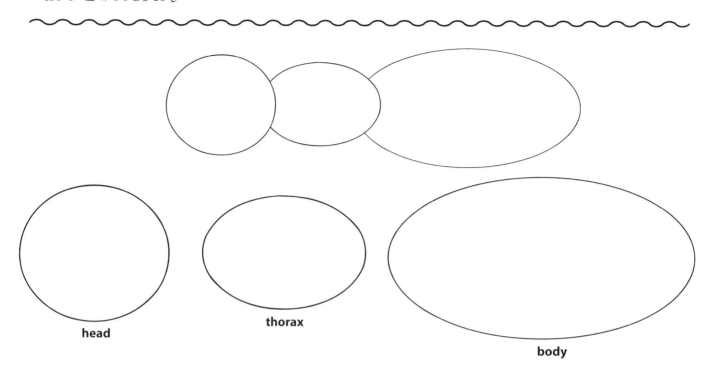

head

thorax

body

Grasshopper Patterns

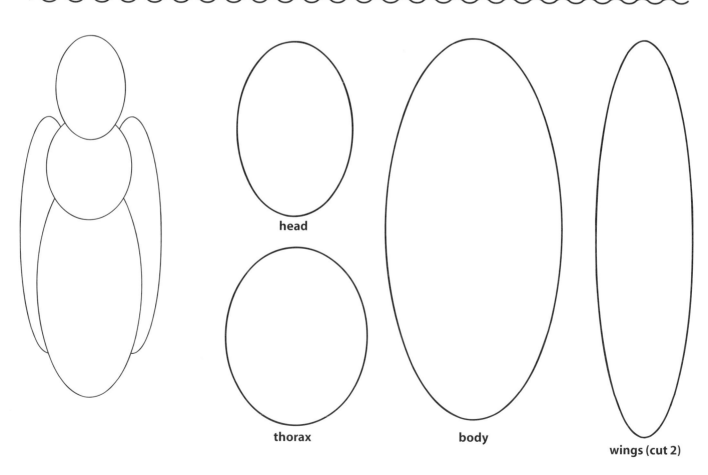

head

thorax

body

wings (cut 2)

The Blind Men and the Elephant

Programming Ideas

Theme: Elephants

Setting the Scene

Ask the children to name the five senses. Explain that the story you are about to read is about six blind men. Do they know which sense they are missing?

Story

The Blind Men and the Elephant
by Karen Backstein

After reading the story, blindfold three children and have them guess different objects. Read some books on the senses such as *The Five Senses* or *How Animals See Things*.

Puppets

Make pencil topper elephant puppets (page 19) and read other elephant stories such as *The Elephant's Wrestling Match, Alistair's Elephant, Elympics, The Story of Babar, Ella, Tacky in Trouble* or *Horton Hatches the Egg*.

Activities

Art

Create an elephant mosaic by enlarging an elephant picture and using scraps of paper to decorate it.

Geography and Cooking

Explain how the story takes place in India. Locate India on a map. Explain that Indian food uses a lot of spices. Ask if any of the children can name some spices. Bring in some spices (such as cloves) and grind them with a mortar and pestle. Let the children smell the different scents.

Math

Discuss how the elephant was strong enough to carry six men. Have everyone guess how much six children might weigh. Bring in a scale and weigh some volun-teers. Guess the weight of other objects, and then see how close the guesses were.

Movement

Ask the children to move like an elephant. Move like other animals. Play "Simon Says" using animal movements.

Research

Read books like *Elephants* to learn more about elephants.

Science

Discuss the statement: "Although these men could not see, they learned about the world in many ways." Explain that perhaps the men used their other senses better than people with sight do. Even with sight, people need magnifiers to see things that are invisible without magnifiers. Ask if anyone can name the scientific instrument that lets you see very tiny things. (*Microscope.*) Ask if anyone can name the scientific instrument that lets you see things very far away. (*Telescope.*) Read *The Microscope* and *Stargazers* and let the children use a microscope and telescope, then read *How to Catch an Elephant* and look at the pictures in *Hidden Worlds* for fun.

Books

Folktale Versions

Backstein, Karen. *The Blind Men and the Elephant.* Scholastic, 1992. Six blind men have different ideas of what an elephant is like.

Young, Ed. *Seven Blind Mice.* Scholastic, 1992. Seven blind mice discover "Something" and try to decide what it is.

Related Reading

Brunhoff, Jean de. *The Story of Babar: The Little Elephant.* Random House, 1933. The famous story of the little elephant.

Fowler, Allan. *How Animals See Things*. Children's Press, 1998. A brief description of how animals (and people) see.

Gibbons, Gail. *Stargazers*. Holiday House, 1992. A brief description of constellations and telescopes.

Hewitt, Sally. *The Five Senses*. Children's Press, 1999. A description of the senses with simple activities.

Kelsey, Elin. *Elephants*. Grolier, 1988. A description of elephants and activities such as keeping cool.

Kennedy, X. J. *Elympics*. Philomel Books, 1999. Poems of elephants competing at sports.

Kramer, Stephen. *Hidden Worlds: Looking Through a Scientist's Microscope*. Houghton Mifflin, 2001. A description of scientists and the microscopes they use to study tiny things.

Kumin, Maxine. *The Microscope*. HarperTrophy, 1968. A rhymed introduction to Anton Leeuwenhoek's discoveries.

Lester, Helen. *Tacky in Trouble*. Houghton Mifflin, 1998. Tacky the Penguin surfs to an island and must convince an elephant he is a penguin.

Peet, Bill. *Ella*. Houghton Mifflin, 1964. A circus elephant learns to be grateful for her friends and circus life after she misses the train.

Sadler, Marilyn. *Alistair's Elephant*. Prentice-Hall, 1983. An elephant follows Alistair home from the zoo.

Schwartz, Amy. *How to Catch an Elephant*. DK Publishing, 1999. A humorous look at catching an elephant with items such as a telescope and raisins.

Seuss, Dr. *Horton Hatches the Egg*. Random House, 1940. Horton hatches a bird's egg even though he is an elephant.

Sierra, Judy. *The Elephant's Wrestling Match*. Lodestar Books, 1992. The mighty elephant challenges animals great and small to a wrestling match.

Elephant Puppet Patterns

Materials:

- crayons
- scissors
- pencils
- black or gray yarn
- tape or stapler
- hole punch

Directions:

1. Color the elephants and cut them out. Make sure students do not cut the tab off.

2. Cut a piece of yarn approximately 2" in length. Fray it at the end. Attach the yarn tail with a staple or tape.

3. Punch out the holes to fit over a pencil head and fold them back on the line.

4. Push a pencil through the holes.

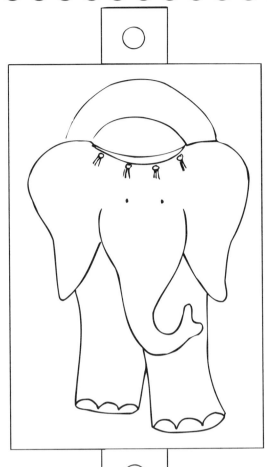

The Fisherman and His Wife

Programming Ideas

Theme: Fish

Setting the Scene

Dress as a fisherman. Ask if anyone fishes. Discuss fishing and explain that the story is about a poor fisherman and his wife who lived by the sea.

Story

The Magic Fish by Freya Littledale

After reading the story, ask the children what they would wish for. Read *The Fish Who Could Wish, Minas and the Fish* or *At the Wish of the Fish* and talk about the wishes used in those stories. Enlarge the fish pictures (page 23) and hand out various pictures. Title a bulletin board "Wish Upon a Fish" and post the fish after the children have written or drawn a wish on their fish.

Note: *The Magic Fish* is currently out of print, but it was available through the local public library. Secondary choices, in print as of publication, are the Wells version (which varies from the original) and the Cole version (lengthy for young children but a couple of the wife's later wishes could be left out).

Puppets

Make the story cubes (page 22). Read the story again as the children color and cut out the cubes. Tell the story using the cube. Then ask for a volunteer to come up and tell the story using the cube. If desired, make the squares into separate puppets for storytelling.

Activities

Aquarium

Keep an aquarium in the classroom or have small groups design and make underwater scene dioramas.

Folklore

Discuss the fish's statement that he is a prince. Do you think he is a human prince or a fish prince? Explain that many stories have people magically changed into animals (and even some animals that are magically changed into people). Can the children name any such stories? (For example: "Beauty and the Beast," "Cinderella," "The Frog Prince"). Read stories the children suggest or try *Prince Cinders, The Dragon Prince* or *The Frog Prince—Continued.*

Math

Give each child several goldfish. Do addition and subtraction problems as a class before letting the children eat the goldfish as a snack. Read *The Biggest Fish* or *How Many Fish?* for more math reinforcement.

Music

Sing songs that have to do with water such as "My Bonnie Lies Over the Ocean," "Three Little Fishies (Itty Bitty Poo)," "Yellow Submarine" or "Row, Row, Row Your Boat."

Research and Reading

Read and look through books like *Fish Faces, Amazing Fish* or *Fish Do the Strangest Things* to see different kinds of fish. Younger children can pick a favorite fish, draw it and share the reason for their choice or an interesting fact about their choice. Older children might research fish and write their own version of the folktale using settings appropriate to their choice of fish. Read other fish stories for fun such as *The Rainbow Fish, Big Al* or *A Fish Out of Water.*

Science

Ask: What do most living things need? After discussion, read *What Is a Living Thing?* or try some of the activities in *Living Things.* Discuss what fish need and how they get it. Read *Fish* or *What Makes a Fish?*

Books

Folktale Versions

Cole, Joanna (ed.). *Best-Loved Folktales of the World.* Doubleday, 1982. A collection of 200 folktales from around the world.

Demi. *The Magic Gold Fish: A Russian Folktale.* Henry Holt & Company, 1995. A fisherman's wife keeps asking for more from a magic fish.

Littledale, Freya. *The Magic Fish.* Scholastic, 1985. A fisherman's wife keeps asking for more from a magic fish.

Spear, Laurinda. *The Fisherman and His Wife.* Rizzoli, 1992. A fisherman's wife keeps asking for more from a magic dolphin.

Wells, Rosemary. *The Fisherman and His Wife.* Dial, 1998. A cat's wife keeps asking for more from a magic fish.

Related Reading

Bush, John, and Korky Paul. *The Fish Who Could Wish.* Kane/Miller, 1991. All of a fish's wishes come true, including his last one.

Clements, Andrew. *Big Al.* Scholastic, 1988. Big Al, the friendly but scary-looking fish, finally gets friends.

Cohen, Caron Lee. *How Many Fish?* HarperCollins, 1998. Fish and children play in the bay.

Cole, Babette. *Prince Cinders.* Putnam & Grosset, 1987. A fairy transforms a prince so that he can attend a disco.

Hornblow, Leonora, and Arthur Hornblow. *Fish Do the Strangest Things.* Random House, 1989. A look at 17 fish.

Kalman, Bobbie. *What Is a Living Thing?* Crabtree Publishing, 1999. An introduction to living things and their characteristics.

Keenan, Sheila. *The Biggest Fish.* Scholastic, 1996. The mayor of Littletown has a contest to locate the biggest fish.

Lewis, J. Patrick. *At the Wish of the Fish: A Russian Folktale.* Atheneum Books, 1999. A magic pike grants a man's wishes.

Ling, Mary. *Amazing Fish.* Knopf, 1991. Describes different groups of fish.

Mason, Adrienne. *Living Things.* Kids Can Press, 1998. Activities that demonstrate how living things need food, air and habitats.

Palmer, Helen. *A Fish Out of Water.* Beginner Books, 1961. A young boy learns that he should not feed his pet fish too much.

Pastuchiv, Olga. *Minas and the Fish.* Houghton Mifflin, 1997. A fish grants Minas's wish to become big and learn to swim.

Pfister, Marcus. *The Rainbow Fish.* North-South Books, 1992. Rainbow Fish learns the importance of sharing.

Richardson, Joy. *Fish.* Franklin Watts, 1993. A description of fish and their characteristics.

Scieszka, Jon. *The Frog Prince—Continued.* Viking, 1991. A prince and a princess rediscover happiness.

Stone, Lynn M. *What Makes a Fish?* Rourke, 1997. A description of fish, including where they live and their importance to people.

Wu, Norbert. *Fish Faces.* Henry Holt & Company, 1993. Photographs of interesting ocean fish.

Yep, Laurence. *The Dragon Prince: A Chinese Beauty and the Beast Tale.* HarperCollins, 1997. A girl agrees to marry a dragon to save her father.

The Fisherman and His Wife Cube Pattern

Materials:

- crayons or markers
- scissors
- card stock or heavier paper

Directions:

1. Photocopy the patterns (enlarge them if desired).

2. Color the patterns.

3. Cut the patterns out.

4. Fold the patterns to form a cube (taping may be necessary).

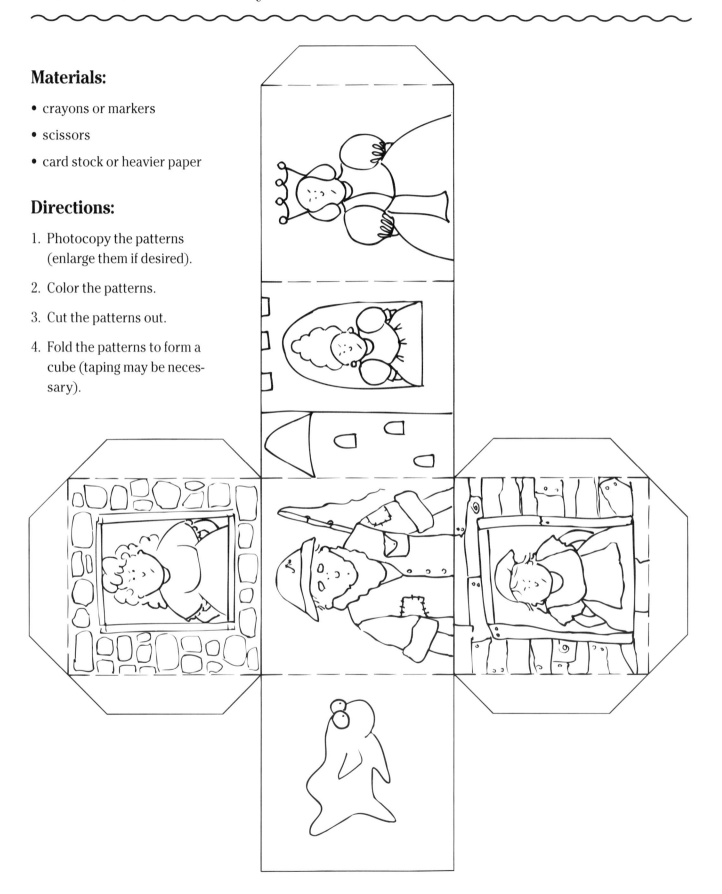

Fish Pictures

Goldilocks and the Three Bears

Programming Ideas

Theme: Bears

Setting the Scene

Bring in three cushions or pillows. Place one on a chair, sit on it, then get up saying, "This cushion is too hard!" Try another and say, "This cushion is too soft!" Try another and say, "This cushion is just right!" Have some students try the cushions. Have the children guess which story you are going to read.

Story

Goldilocks and the Three Bears
by Valeri Gorbachev

After reading the standard version, read variations of the story such as *Dusty Locks and the Three Bears, Goldilocks and the Three Hares* or *Somebody and the Three Blairs.*

Puppets

Copy a set of stand-up puppets (pages 26–27) for each student and several blank stand-ups (page 28) for older students to use for drawing "props" such as bowls, chairs and beds on the blank stand-ups. Tell the story using the figures. Some children might want to use a dollhouse or make their own cottages out of shoeboxes.

Activities

Character Education

Ask the children if they thought Goldilocks did something wrong. What is something you can do after you make a mistake or do something wrong? *(Apologize—in person or in writing.)* Write apology letters as though you are Goldilocks. Read *The Jolly Postman* for sample letters from several folktale characters. Read *Goldilocks Returns* and discuss.

Cooking

Ask: What is porridge? *(Porridge is boiled cereal, like oatmeal, usually eaten with milk.)* Have a taste test using several kinds of hot cereal. Chart the results.

Movement

Take a nature walk, play musical chairs or play a game of "Wake the Bear." To play the game: One child hides his or her eyes while another person is designated as the bear. The bear and other children put their heads on their desks pretending sleep. The original child comes back and taps five children. If he or she taps the bear, the bear stands up and roars. The child gets to play again while the bear chooses the next bear. If the child does not tap the bear, then he chooses the next person to hide his or her eyes and the bear chooses the next bear.

Music

Learn songs and rhymes about bears such as "The Bear Went Over the Mountain," "Going on a Bear Hunt," and "Teddy Bear, Teddy Bear." Listen to a recording of "The Teddy Bears' Picnic."

Research and Reading

Read books like *Bears* (by Holmes or Stone) or *Black Bears* to learn more about bears. Then read stories like *The Bear on the Moon, Little Bear, Bear Snores On* or *You and Me, Little Bear.*

Science

Discuss how the bears and Goldilocks needed food. Ask: What do living things need? Read *What Is a Living Thing?* Read *Eat Well* or *The Edible Pyramid* to learn more about the food people should eat. Read *Dig and Sow!* to learn more about what plants need.

Books

Folktale Versions

Brett, Jan. *Goldilocks and the Three Bears.* Putnam, 1987. A young girl enters the home of three bears.

Cauley, Lorinda Bryan. *Goldilocks and the Three Bears.* Putnam, 1981. A young girl enters the home of three bears.

Ernst, Lisa Campbell. *Goldilocks Returns.* Simon & Schuster, 2000. Fifty years later, Goldilocks returns to the bears' home to fix what she broke.

Gorbachev, Valeri. *Goldilocks and the Three Bears.* North-South Books, 2001. A young girl enters the home of three bears.

Lowell, Susan. *Dusty Locks and the Three Bears.* Henry Holt & Company, 2001. Way out West, a young girl enters the home of three grizzly bears.

Marshall, James. *Goldilocks and the Three Bears.* Dial, 1988. A young girl enters the home of three bears.

Petach, Heidi. *Goldilocks and the Three Hares.* Putnam, 1995. A young girl enters the home of three hares.

Rosales, Melodye Benson. *Leola and the Honeybears.* Scholastic, 1999. An African American retelling of "Goldilocks and the Three Bears."

Ross, Tony. *Goldilocks and the Three Bears.* Overlook Press, 1992. A young girl enters the home of three bears.

Stevens, Janet. *Goldilocks and the Three Bears.* Holiday House, 1986. A young girl enters the home of three bears.

Tolhurst, Marilyn. *Somebody and the Three Blairs.* Orchard Books, 1991. A young bear enters the Blair home.

Turkle, Brinton. *Deep in the Forest.* Dutton, 1976. A wordless picture book of a young bear entering a frontier cabin.

Related Reading

Ahlberg, Janet, and Allan Ahlberg. *The Jolly Postman Or, Other People's Letters.* Little, Brown and Company, 1986. A postman delivers several letters from folktale characters.

Helmer, Diana Star. *Black Bears.* PowerKids Press, 1997. A description of bears and their characteristics.

Holmes, Kevin J. *Bears.* Bridgestone Books, 1998. A description of bears and their characteristics.

Kalman, Bobbie. *What Is a Living Thing?* Crabtree Publishing, 1999. An introduction to living things and their characteristics.

Leedy, Loreen. *The Edible Pyramid—Good Eating Every Day.* Holiday House, 1994. Customers visit the Edible Pyramid restaurant.

Lobb, Janice. *Dig And Sow! How Do Plants Grow?* Kingfisher, 2000. Explanations and activities that answer questions such as "Do plants eat and drink?"

Minarik, Else Holmelund. *Little Bear.* Harper & Row, 1957. Four short stories featuring Little Bear and Mother Bear.

Rosen, Michael. *We're Going on a Bear Hunt.* Margaret K. McElderry Books, 1989. Hunters go through many obstacles before finding a bear.

Royston, Angela. *Eat Well.* Heinemann Library, 2000. Discusses the food pyramid and various nutrients.

Ryder, Joanne. *The Bear on the Moon.* William Morrow & Co., 1991. A story of how a bear went to the moon and sent some of its land down to Earth.

Sivulich, Sandra Stroner. *I'm Going on a Bear Hunt.* Dutton, 1973. A boy goes through many obstacles before finding a bear.

Stone, Lynn M. *Bears.* Rourke, 1993. A description of bears and their characteristics.

Waddell, Martin. *You and Me, Little Bear.* Candlewick Press, 1996. Little Bear and Big Bear do chores before they play together.

Wilson, Karma. *Bear Snores On.* Margaret K. McElderry Books, 2002. Several animals find shelter in a bear's cave before waking him up.

Goldilocks and the Three Bears Puppet Patterns

Materials:

- card stock or heavier paper
- crayons or markers
- scissors

Directions:

1. Photocopy the patterns (enlarge them if desired).

2. Color the patterns and cut them out.

3. Fold the patterns on the dotted lines.

Goldilocks

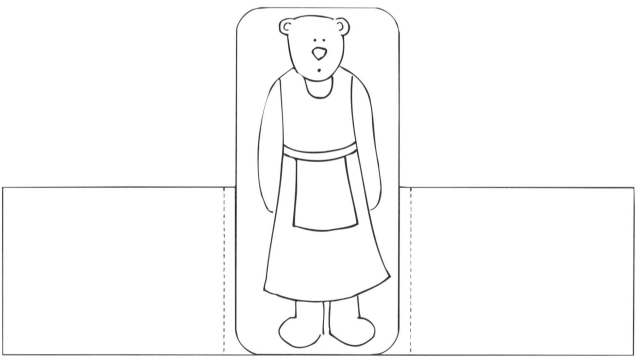

Mama Bear

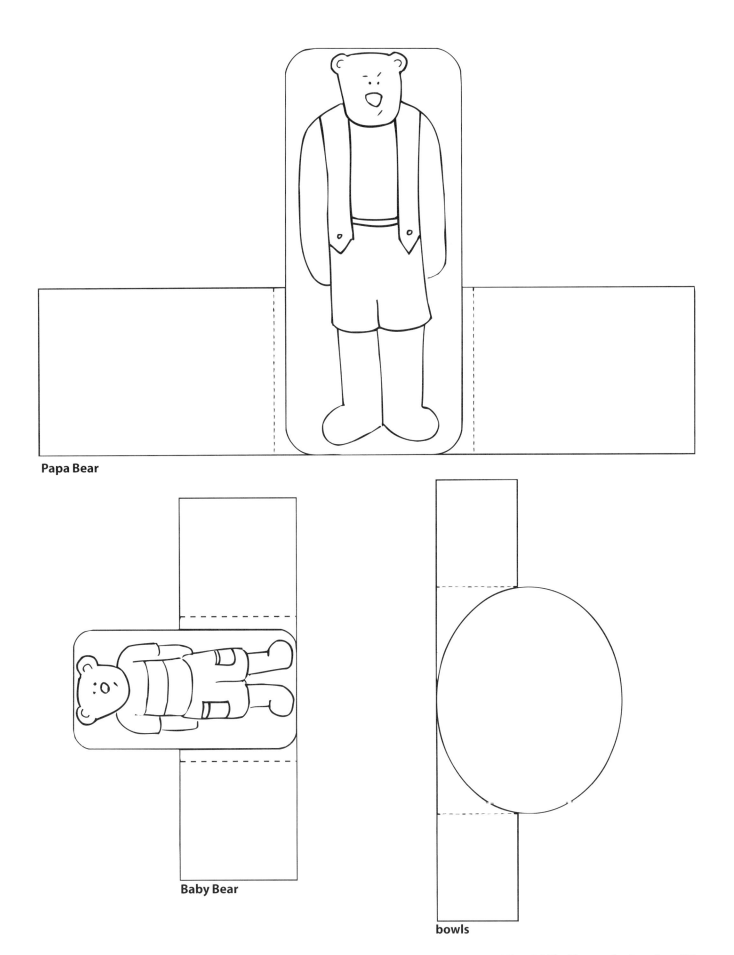

Papa Bear

Baby Bear

bowls

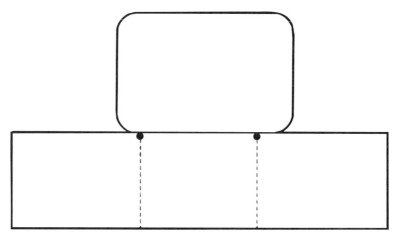

chairs/beds — cut along tab to dots

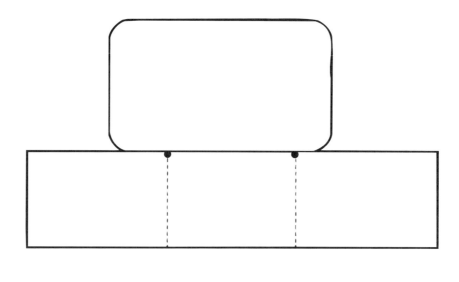

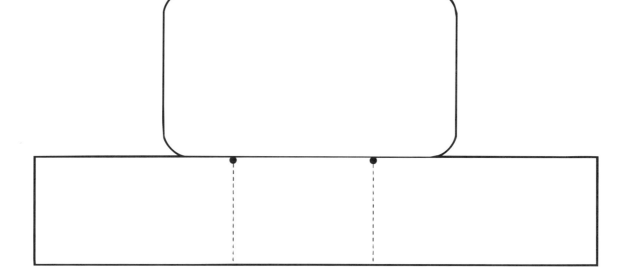

Henny Penny

Programming Ideas

Theme: Birds

Setting the Scene

Ask the children if they like names that rhyme. (For example: Mark Lark, Silly Willy, Polly Wolly, Susie Qusie, etc.) Explain that the story you are about to read has names that rhyme. See if anyone can fill in the blanks: Henny ____, Cocky ____, Ducky ____, Goosey ____, Turkey ____ and Foxy ____.

Story

Henny Penny by H. Werner Zimmerman

After reading and discussing the story, read Kellogg's *Chicken Little* and discuss the similarities and differences between the two stories.

Puppets

Make one set of puppets (page 31) for teacher use. Ask students to come up and act out the story as it is read using the puppets. Afterwards, students can each make a Henny Penny puppet and make up stories.

Activities

Art

Some versions of the story show the birds wearing pans and other items as hats to protect themselves from the falling sky. Look at *Hats Hats Hats* or *Hats Off to Hats!* and design hats for various folktale characters or for those days when the sky is falling.

Bird Watching

Have the children look for birds at school and at home. Identify them. Read *Counting Is for the Birds* to see common backyard birds and get some math reinforcement. If possible, get a birdsong recording and match the songs to the birds previously identified. Make bird feeders by putting chilled peanut butter on pinecones and rolling the pinecones in birdseed.

Bulletin Board

Title the board "Great Oaks from Little Acorns Grow." Enlarge the oak tree (page 32) for the bulletin board. Copy an acorn for each child (page 32), enlarging it if necessary. Write the child's name and something great they would like to do or become when they grow up. Put the acorns on the board. Make birds to put in the tree.

Folklore

Henny Penny and her friends act foolishly. Folktales featuring silly people are sometimes called "noodle tales." Read *There Is a Carrot in My Ear and Other Noodle Tales.*

Research and Reading

Read books like *What Is a Bird?* or *Birds A to Z* to learn more about birds. Read *The Ugly Duckling, The Story About Ping, Tacky the Penguin, Rainbow Crow, Make Way For Ducklings* or *Good Morning, Chick* for fun.

Science

Discuss how the animals were friends and how one character's actions influenced another's actions. Read *The Dancing Deer and the Foolish Hunter* or *Who Eats What?* and discuss the interdependence of life. Make posters showing some aspect of this interdependence.

Books

Folktale Versions

Crawford, K. Michael. *Chicken Little.* Ideals, 1999. Chicken Little and friends meet a fox on their way to tell the king the sky is falling.

Galdone, Paul. *Henny Penny.* Clarion Books, 1968. Henny Penny and her friends meet a fox on their way to tell the king the sky is falling.

Kellogg, Steven. *Chicken Little.* HarperCollins, 1985. Chicken Little and friends meet a fox on their way to tell the police the sky is falling.

Scieszka, Jon. *The Stinky Cheese Man and Other Fairly Stupid Tales.* Scholastic, 1992. Ten tales with a twist, including "Chicken Licken."

Wattenberg, Jane. *Henny-Penny.* Scholastic, 2000. A contemporary retelling of the story where Henny Penny and her friends meet a fox on their way to tell the king the sky is falling.

Zimmermann, H. Werner. *Henny Penny.* Scholastic, 1989. Henny Penny and her friends meet a fox on their way to tell the king the sky is falling.

Related Reading

Andersen, Hans Christian. *The Ugly Duckling.* Morrow Junior Books, 1999. An ugly duckling discovers that he is really a swan.

Corbett, Sara. *Hats Off to Hats!* Children's Press, 1995. A look at hats and why people wear them.

DeGezelle, Terri. *Birds A to Z.* A+ Books, 2000. Photographs and interesting facts about 26 kinds of birds.

Flack, Marjorie. *The Story About Ping.* Scholastic, 1933. A duck becomes separated from his family along the Yangtze River.

Ginsburg, Mirra. *Good Morning, Chick.* Scholastic, 1980. A chick hatches and explores the barnyard.

Kalman, Bobbie. *What Is a Bird?* Crabtree Publishing, 1999. A description of birds and some of their characteristics.

Kleven, Elisa. *The Dancing Deer and the Foolish Hunter.* Dutton Children's Books, 2002. A hunter wants to sell a dancing deer to the circus, but the deer needs to hear birds singing to dance.

Lauber, Patricia. *Who Eats What? Food Chains and Food Webs.* HarperCollins, 1995. Explains how plants, animals and people are interdependent.

Lester, Helen. *Tacky the Penguin.* Houghton Mifflin, 1988. Tacky saves his friends from hunters.

Mazzola, Frank Jr. *Counting Is for the Birds.* Charlesbridge, 1997. A backyard bird counting book.

McCloskey, Robert. *Make Way for Ducklings.* Scholastic, 1941. Mrs. Mallard and her ducklings have an adventure in the city as they walk to their new home.

Morris, Ann. *Hats Hats Hats.* Lothrop, Lee & Shepard Books, 1989. Photographs of hats from around the world.

Schwartz, Alvin. *There Is a Carrot in My Ear and Other Noodle Tales.* HarperTrophy, 1982. Six stories about a silly family.

Van Laan, Nancy. *Rainbow Crow: A Lenape Tale.* Dragonfly Books, 1989. Crow brings the gift of fire down to the cold world.

Henny Penny Puppet Patterns

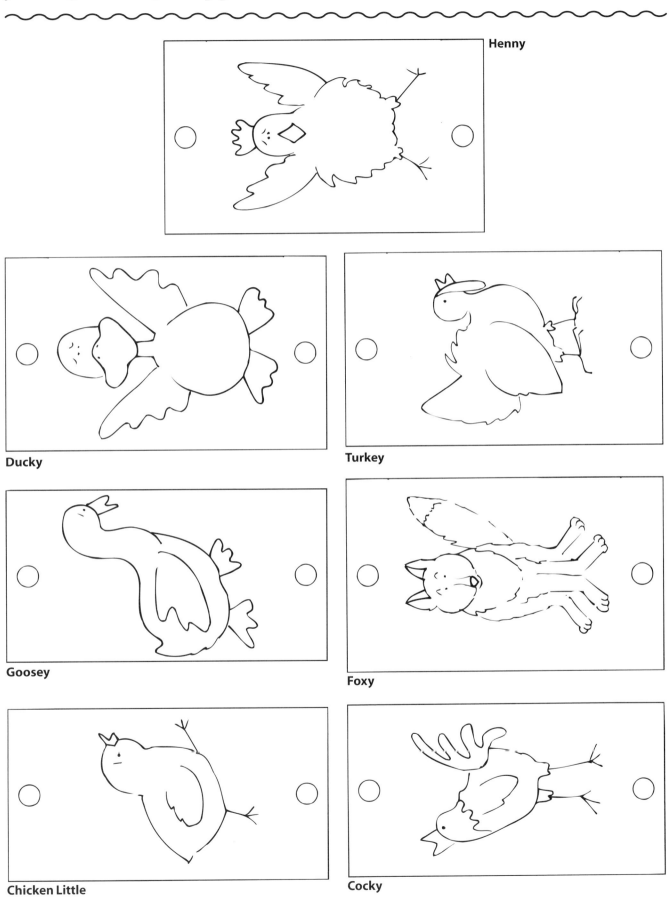

Henny

Ducky

Turkey

Goosey

Foxy

Chicken Little

Cocky

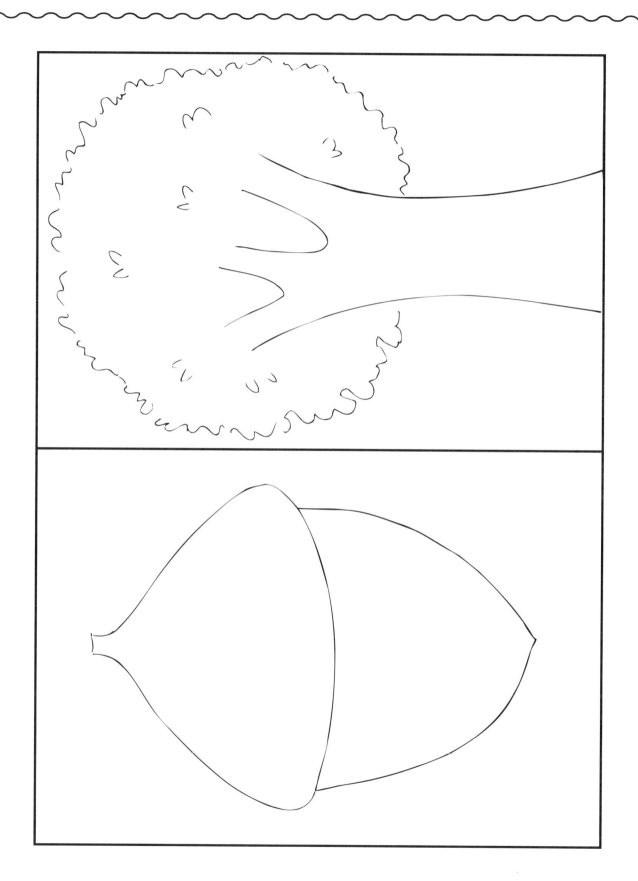

How Brer Rabbit Lost His Fine Bushy Tail

Programming Ideas

Theme: Rabbits

Setting the Scene

Say the word "brother" in several different languages: *hermano* (Spanish), *frère* (French), *bruder* (German) and *fratello* (Italian). Ask the children if they know what word you are saying. See if anyone knows the word in any other languages. Then explain that the story you are about to read uses the word "brer" which is short for "brother."

Story

How Brer Rabbit Lost His Fine Bushy Tail
by Karima Amin

After reading the story, tell the children how journalist Joel Chandler Harris collected the stories by listening and writing the stories down exactly as he heard them. He started publishing the stories in the 1870s. Discuss the oral tradition of folktales. Ask the children if they remember any baby stories told about themselves or other members of the family. Write down and/or illustrate a family story.

Puppets

Make fan puppets (page 35). Summarize the main points of the story and then have the children improvise the story in pairs or by themselves using the puppets. Ask volunteers to perform for the class.

Activities

Science

Discuss how Brer Rabbit and his friends live in the same area but have different adaptations for survival. Read *Claws, Coats, and Camouflage, What Do You Do When Something Wants to Eat You?* or *How Do Animals Adapt?* and discuss different features that help animals (and plants) survive.

Research and Reading

Read books like *Rabbits, Rabbits and More Rabbits* and *Rabbits Have Bunnies* to learn more about rabbits. Read *The Very Bad Bunny, The Tale of Peter Rabbit* or *Rabbit Makes a Monkey of Lion* for fun.

Astronomy

Ask if Brer Rabbit would have had moonlight all night as he fished. Read books such as *Does the Moon Change Shape?* or *So That's How the Moon Changes Shape!* to learn more about the moon's phases. Look at *Find the Constellations* to learn more about constellations or to locate the Hare constellation. Draw Brer Rabbit fishing at night with different constellations and the moon at different phases. Post.

Art

Make rabbits (page 37) by cutting out paper or fabric. Read *Let's Make Rabbits* and *Nothing Sticks Like a Shadow.*

Geography

Explain that Brer Rabbit is an African American folktale character. Locate Africa on a map and a globe. Compare its location with that of the United States. Then compare the continents. Write the names of the continents on slips of paper and put them in a container. Ask a volunteer to draw a slip and try to locate the continent on the map or globe.

Folklore

Read other Brer Rabbit tales. Discuss how stories sometimes give animals attributes they do not really have.

Books

Folktale Versions

Amin, Karima. *The Adventures of Brer Rabbit and Friends.* Family Learning, 1999. A retelling of some of the stories collected by Joel Chandler Harris.

Lester, Julius. *The Tales of Uncle Remus—The Adventures of Brer Rabbit.* Dial, 1987. A collection of over 40 Brer Rabbit stories. (**Note:** Does not contain "How Brer Rabbit Lost His Fine Bushy Tail.")

Weiss, Jaqueline Shachter. *Young Brer Rabbit and Other Trickster Tales from the Americas.* Stemmer House, 1985. Brer Rabbit stories from Venezuela, Brazil, Panama, Martinique, Puerto Rico and Colombia. (**Note:** Does not contain "How Brer Rabbit Lost His Fine Bushy Tail.")

Related Reading

Aardema, Verna. *Rabbit Makes a Monkey of Lion.* Puffin Pied Piper, 1989. Rabbit and his friends trick Lion after they try to eat his honey.

Fowler, Allan. *So That's How the Moon Changes Shape!* Children's Press, 1991. A simple description of how the moon appears to change shape.

Gibbons, Gail. *Rabbits, Rabbits and More Rabbits.* Holiday House, 2000. A description of rabbits and their close relative, the hare.

Goldish, Meish. *Does the Moon Change Shape?* Raintree Steck-Vaughn, 1989. A simple description of how the moon appears, an activity to demonstrate its changes and a calendar showing the moon's phases.

Goodman, Susan E. *Claws, Coats, and Camouflage: The Way Animals Fit into their World.* Lerner Publishing Group, 2001. Describes how different animals adapt, fit in, stay safe, get food and make a new generation.

Jenkins, Steve. *What Do You Do When Something Wants to Eat You?* Houghton Mifflin, 1997. Describes how some animals escape from danger.

Kalman, Bobbie. *How Do Animals Adapt?* Crabtree Publishing, 2000. Describes animal adaptations for survival.

Lionni, Leo. *Let's Make Rabbits: A Fable.* Dragonfly Books, 1982. A pencil and a pair of scissors each make rabbits.

McDermott, Gerald. *Zomo the Rabbit: A Trickster Tale from West Africa.* Harcourt, 1992. Clever Zomo performs three tasks to gain wisdom.

Potter, Beatrix. *The Tale of Peter Rabbit.* Warne, 1987. Peter is naughty and goes into Mr. McGregor's garden.

Rey, H. A. *Find the Constellations.* Houghton Mifflin, 1976. A description of constellations including drawings of how the night sky looks at different times of the year—with and without the constellations drawn.

Sadler, Marilyn. *The Very Bad Bunny.* Random House, 1984. P. J. Funnybunny appears to be bad until his family meets a very bad bunny.

Stone, Lynn M. *Rabbits Have Bunnies.* Compass Point Books, 2000. A description of newborn bunnies and their growth into adulthood.

Tompert, Ann. *Nothing Sticks Like a Shadow.* Houghton Mifflin, 1984. Rabbit tries to get rid of his shadow and is sad when he thinks he did.

How Brer Rabbit Lost His Fine Bushy Tail Puppet Fans

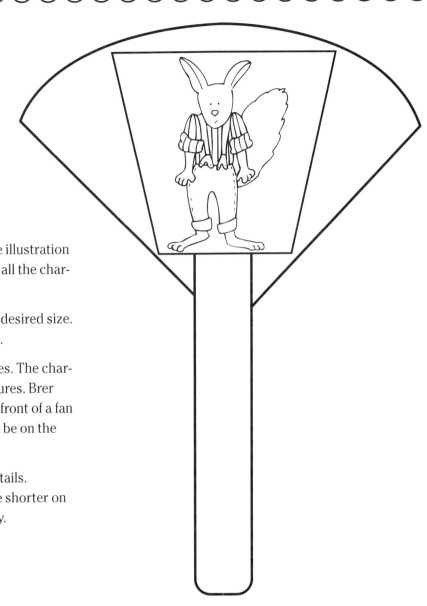

Materials:

- paper plates
- popsicle sticks
- crayons
- paste or staples
- cotton balls*

Directions:

1. Cut the paper plates into quarters (see illustration below). You will need five quarters for all the characters.

2. Enlarge the patterns on page 36 to the desired size. Color the characters and cut them out.

3. Paste the characters to the paper plates. The character of Brer Rabbit will have two pictures. Brer Rabbit with the long tail will be on the front of a fan and Brer Rabbit with the short tail will be on the back of the same fan.

* Children can paste on cotton balls for tails. Remember—Brer Rabbit's tail must be shorter on the second picture to go with the story.

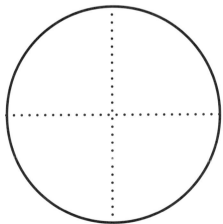

Brer Rabbit

Fox

Terrapin

Bear

Raccoon

Rabbit Patterns

The Monkey and the Crocodile

Programming Ideas

Theme: Monkeys and Crocodiles

Setting the Scene

Ask: How many of you can run fast? Are you the fastest of everyone you know or is there someone faster than you? Ask: How many of you are strong? Are you the strongest of everyone you know or is there someone stronger? Ask: How many of you are cunning? Explain that in the story you are about to read, a crocodile thinks he is more cunning than the monkey. (As a class, figure out what cunning means after reading the story.)

Story

The Monkey and the Crocodile by Paul Galdone

Discuss alligators and crocodiles after reading the story. If possible, read *Gator or Croc?* Ask: Should everyone always be careful around these animals? Why? Read other stories that show that you should be careful of them, such as *Five Little Monkeys Sitting in a Tree,* Marshall's *Red Riding Hood* or *Petite Rouge.*

Puppets

Make crocodile and monkey puppets (page 40). The children can act out the story using the puppets while you read the story again.

Activities

Game

Have a learning center, which features a Barrel of Monkeys (available commercially) or have a contest where the teacher is "the crocodile" and asks for a volunteer to be "the monkey" and stand in the back of the class. The teacher asks questions pertaining to curriculum while the student takes a giant step forward with each correct answer. The student earns some sort of treat if he or she reaches the front of the classroom.

Geography

Discuss animals that live in rain forests. Read *Predators in the Rain Forest* and *Animals of the Rain Forest* to learn more. Draw pictures or write stories set in a rain forest.

Math

Make several copies of the mango picture (page 43), enlarging it if necessary. Write math equations on one side and the answer on the other. Use as flash cards or put on a bulletin board using the tree pattern (page 32 in Henny Penny chapter). Bring in mangoes and other fruit for math practice and then sample the fruit when finished.

Movement

Draw chalk circles on the pavement to resemble the rocks the monkey jumped on to get to the island. Ask the children to try jumping them. (For fun, put a crocodile figure on the last "rock.") Then teach the children how to play hopscotch.

Research and Reading

Read books like *Monkeys Are a Lot Like Us* to learn more about monkeys. Read *The Best Little Monkeys in the World, Five Little Monkeys Jumping on the Bed* or *Caps For Sale* for fun.

Science

Read *Prehistoric Animals* to learn more about animals that lived long ago, including some, like the crocodile, that still live today. Discuss how some organisms have disappeared over time and how some, like the horse and camel, have changed into the animals we see today. Read *Dinosaur Days* and *Baby Alligator* for more information on dinosaurs and alligators.

Books

Folktale Versions

Cole, Joanna (ed.). *Best-Loved Folktales of the World.* Doubleday, 1982. A collection of 200 folktales from around the world.

Galdone, Paul. *The Monkey and the Crocodile: A Jataka Tale from India.* Clarion Books, 1969. A crocodile tries to catch a monkey.

Tata, Mrudel. *The Monkey and the Crocodile and Other Stories.* Tata Publishing, 1995. Three stories from India.

Related Reading

Artell, Mike. *Petite Rouge: A Cajun Red Riding Hood.* Dial, 2001. A young duck outwits a crocodile with the help of a cat.

Christelow, Eileen. *Five Little Monkeys Jumping on the Bed.* Clarion Books, 1989. Monkeys bump their heads because they jumped on the bed.

Christelow, Eileen. *Five Little Monkeys Sitting in a Tree.* Clarion Books, 1991. Five little monkeys tease a crocodile.

Clarke, Ginjer L. *Baby Alligator.* Grosset & Dunlap, 2000. Drawings and text show a Florida alligator leaving its nest and growing big.

Fowler, Allan. *Gator or Croc?* Children's Press, 1996. A simple description of alligators and crocodiles and the differences between them.

Fowler, Allan. *Monkeys Are a Lot Like Us.* Children's Press, 1995. A simple description of monkeys, how they differ from apes and the difference between New World and Old World monkeys.

Gibbons, Gail. *Prehistoric Animals.* Holiday House, 1988. A brief look at some prehistoric animals.

Marshall, James. *Red Riding Hood.* Puffin Books, 1987. A girl encounters a dangerous wolf.

Milton, Joyce. *Dinosaur Days.* Random House, 1985. A look at life in the time of the dinosaurs.

Pirotta, Saviour. *Predators in the Rain Forest.* Raintree Steck-Vaughn, 1999. A look at predators on the forest floor, in the sky and in the rivers and lakes.

Slobodkina, Esphyr. *Caps for Sale.* HarperCollins, 1947. A peddler tries to get his caps from some monkeys.

Standiford, Natalie. *The Best Little Monkeys in the World.* Random House, 1987. Two monkeys make mischief when the babysitter is not looking.

Woods, Mae. *Animals of the Rain Forest.* ABDO Publishing, 1999. Describes the physical characteristics and behaviors of some rain forest animals.

The Monkey and the Crocodile Puppets

Materials:

- construction paper (yellow, black, green, red, dark brown and light brown)
- scissors
- paste
- lunch bags
- crayons or markers

Directions:

1. Photocopy the monkey/crocodile patterns (pages 41–42) onto heavier paper for tracing, or photocopy them and then color.

2. Trace and cut out the pattern pieces as follows:

   - Green: crocodile head and mouth
   - Yellow: eyes
   - Black: pupils
   - Red: throat
   - Dark brown: monkey head, mouth and ears
   - Light brown: monkey face and inside ears

3. Crocodile

   a. Paste the pupil on the yellow eye.

   b. Paste the eyes on the croc.

   c. Paste the throat on the mouth.

   d. Lift the bottom of the bag and paste the mouth under the bag bottom.

   e. Paste the head on the top of the bag bottom.

   f. With crayons, add a nose and other features.

4. Monkey

   a. Paste the face to the head.

   b. Paste the inner ears on the ears above the paste line.

   c. Paste the ears to the side of the head.

   d. Paste the head to the bag bottom.

   e. Fold one mouth along the dotted line. Paste the mouth to the face with the fold line along the edge of the bag's bottom.

   f. Lift the bottom and paste the second mouth to the bag. Make sure the mouth pieces meet.

   g. Color the eyes.

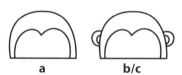

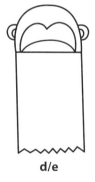  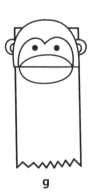

 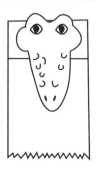

Monkey Patterns

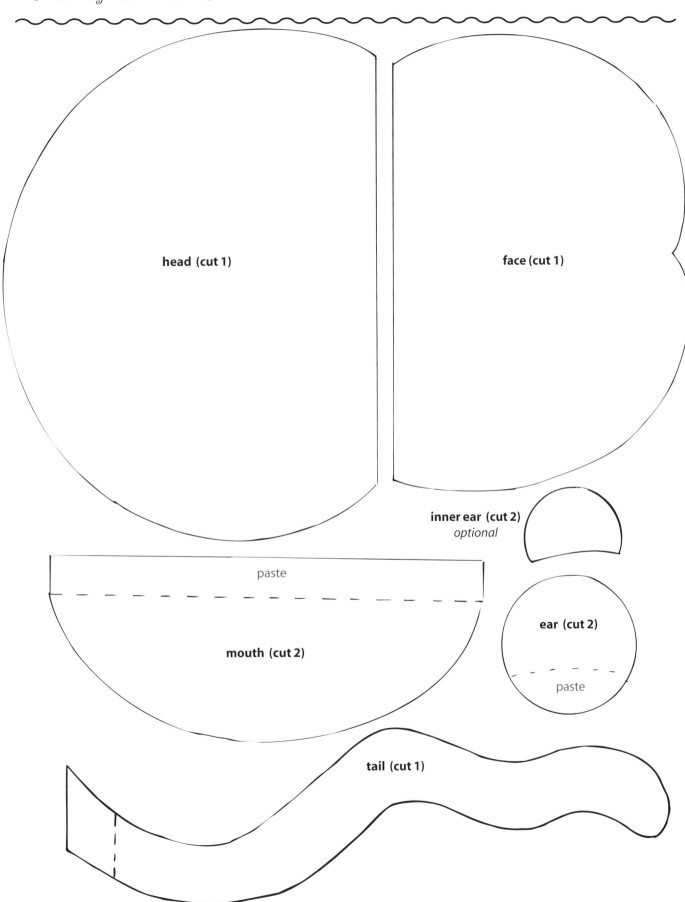

head (cut 1)

face (cut 1)

inner ear (cut 2)
optional

paste

mouth (cut 2)

ear (cut 2)

paste

tail (cut 1)

Crocodile Patterns

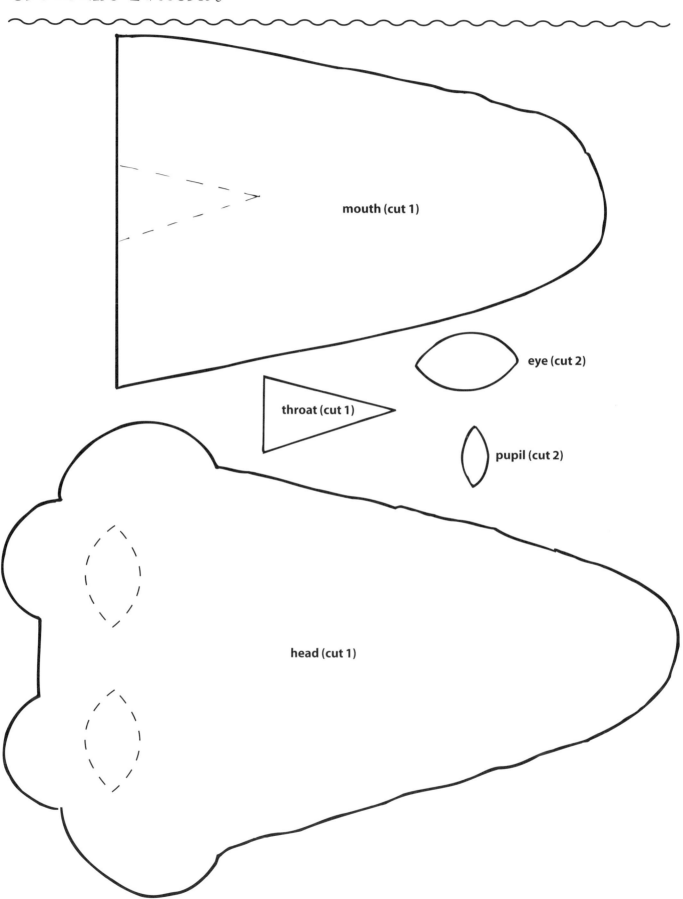

mouth (cut 1)

eye (cut 2)

throat (cut 1)

pupil (cut 2)

head (cut 1)

Mango Pattern

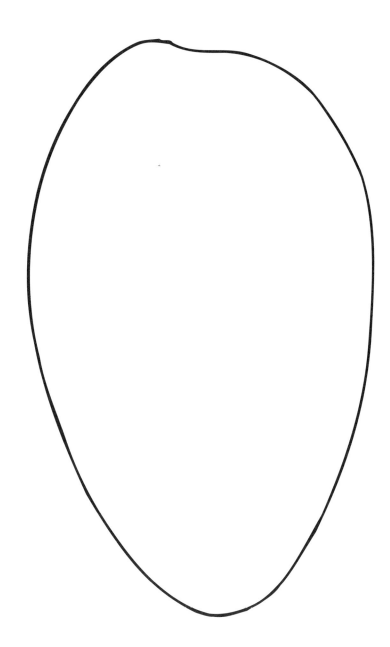

The Three Little Pigs

Programming Ideas

Theme: Pigs

Setting the Scene

Ask the children to watch you. Sit very still, breathing in through your nose and out through your mouth. Ask them if they can tell you what you were doing. (For example: thinking, seeing, breathing, etc.) Discuss the importance of breathing. Have the children each hold up a sheet of paper close to their mouths. Blow. The paper moves easily. Hold it further away. Blow. Hold it as far away as possible. Does it still move? Explain that you are about to read a story where breathing (and blowing) is an important part of the story. Can anyone guess what the story is? (If not, give a hint: "I'll huff and I'll puff...")

Note: Be careful not to hyperventilate.

Story

The Three Little Pigs by Barry Moser

After reading the story, discuss the importance of manners. For example: Would the man have given the straw if the pig had said, "Give me that straw!" Act out how to share materials such as crayons or toys using words and phrases like, "Please" and "Thank You" and "When you are finished, could ..."

Puppets

Make a set of sliding puppets and props (pages 46–47). Tell the story again. Put the string and sliding puppets into a center for the children to use, or have them make their own set to take home.

Activities

Art

Copy the pig face (page 48) onto an overhead transparency. Demonstrate cartooning techniques showing different styles of beards (for the hair on the chinny chin chins), moustaches and hairstyles. Or ask the students to draw their dream homes or dream bedrooms.

Cooking

Make something with turnips or apples or demonstrate how to make butter by putting heavy cream or whipping cream and a pinch of salt in a mason jar and shaking the jar all day (pass the jar around so everyone can have a turn or two).

Learning Center

Have building blocks at a center for building houses. Or put a Pick-Up-Sticks game (available commercially) at the center.

Research and Reading

Read books like *Pigs* or *Smart, Clean Pigs* to learn more about pigs. Read *The Three Pigs, The Amazing Bone* or *Piggie Pie* for fun.

Science

Discuss straw, sticks and bricks. What can they be used for? Discuss how many materials can be used again, sometimes in a different form. Read *Recycle That!* to learn more about recycling.

Telling Time

Make clocks (page 122 in the Gingerbread Man section). Have the children move the big hands and little hands to show the times mentioned in the story. Read *Tick-Tock* and *Clocks and More Clocks.* Sing "Hickory Dickory Dock." Practice using clocks based on the stories and song.

Books

Folktale Versions

Galdone, Paul. *The Three Little Pigs.* Clarion Books, 1970. A pig outwits a wolf.

Hooks, William H. *The Three Little Pigs and the Fox.* Macmillan, 1989. Three little pigs leave home and deal with a fox.

Lowell, Susan. *The Three Little Javelinas.* Northland Publishing, 1992. A version of "The Three Little Pigs" with javelinas and a coyote.

Marshall, James. *The Three Little Pigs.* Dial, 1989. A pig outwits a wolf.

Moser, Barry. *The Three Little Pigs.* Little, Brown and Company, 2001. A pig outwits a wolf.

Rounds, Glen. *Three Little Pigs and the Big Bad Wolf.* Holiday House, 1992. A pig outwits a wolf.

Trivizas, Eugene. *The Three Little Wolves and the Big Bad Pig.* Scholastic, 1993. Three little wolves build houses to protect themselves from the big bad pig.

Related Reading

Anderson, Lena. *Tick-Tock.* R & S Books, 1998. A simple picture book of animal children spending a day from 1 p.m. until midnight.

Bell, Rachael. *Pigs.* Heinemann, 2000. A description of pigs and pig farms.

Fowler, Allan. *Smart, Clean Pigs.* Children's Press, 1993. A simple description of pigs.

Hutchins, Pat. *Clocks and More Clocks.* Aladdin Books, 1970. Mr. Higgins believes his clocks are all wrong.

Palatini, Margie. *Piggie Pie.* Clarion Books, 1995. A witch goes to Old MacDonald's farm to get piggies to make piggie pie.

Robinson, Fay. *Recycle That!* Children's Press, 1995. A simple description of recycling including where paper products, glass and plastics come from.

Steig, William. *The Amazing Bone.* Puffin Books, 1976. Pearl the pig finds an amazing bone that talks and helps save her from a fox.

Wiesner, David. *The Three Pigs.* Clarion Books, 2001. The three pigs from the familiar story interact with other folktale characters.

Three Little Pigs Puppet Directions

Materials:

- string
- scissors
- crayons

Directions:

1. Photocopy the patterns on pages 46–47. Enlarge if desired.
2. Color, cut and fold the patterns in half.
3. Place the folded puppet over string.

The Three Little Pigs Puppet Patterns

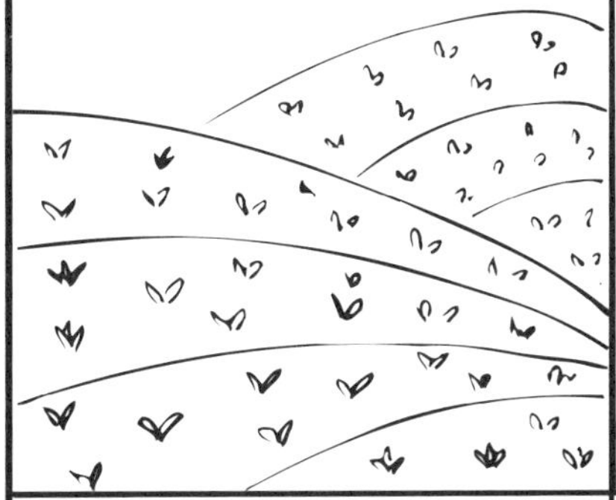

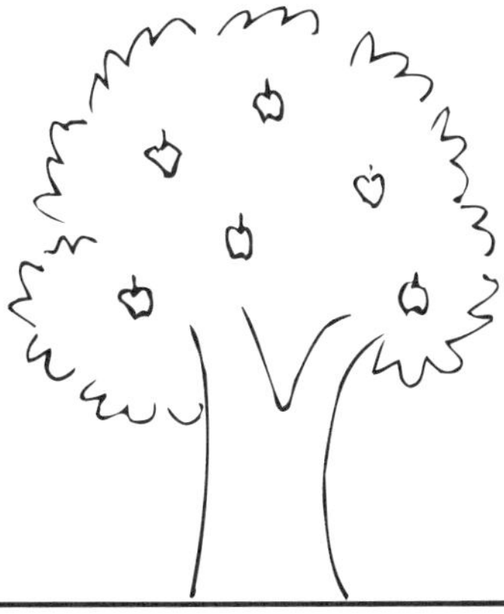

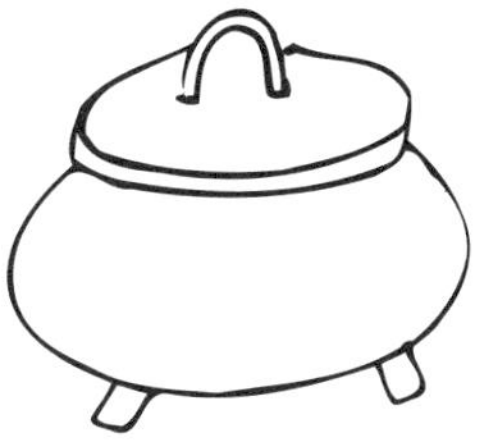

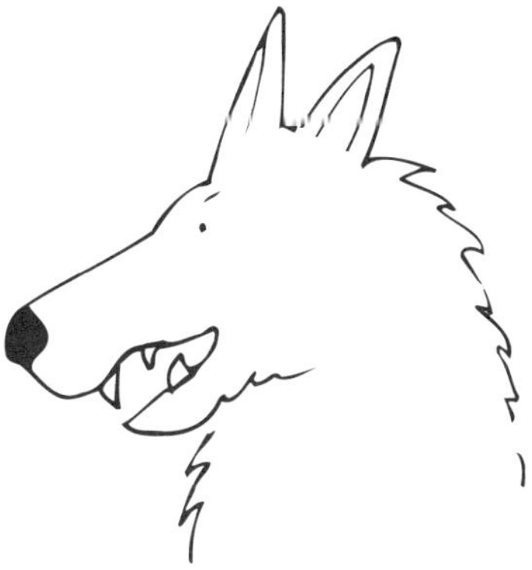

The Tortoise and the Hare

Programming Ideas

Theme: Turtles

Setting the Scene

As a class, brainstorm animals that move quickly, then brainstorm animals that move slowly. Pick one from each category (but not a tortoise and a hare). Ask what would happen if the two animals raced. Ask them to guess which story you are about to read.

Story

The Tortoise and the Hare by Betty Miles

After reading the story, explain that it is one of Aesop's fables. Identify the moral to the story and then read some other fables.

Puppets

Copy the tortoise and hare puppets (page 51) and the racetrack (page 53) onto card stock . Volunteers may have to cut the puppets out for younger children. Read the story while the children act out the story at their desks. Older children may want to create their own "race courses."

Activities

Science

Explain that some animals are similar in how they survive in an environment and some animals are different in how they survive in that same environment. Read *Claws, Coats, and Camouflage* to learn how different animals adapt, fit in, stay safe, get food and make a new generation or read *What Lives in a Shell?* to learn how different animals use shells for protection. Discuss the adaptations of turtles that help them survive, then discuss adaptations of hares/rabbits and other animals.

Research and Reading

Read books like *Turtles Take Their Time, Look Out for Turtles* or *All About Turtles* to learn more about turtles

and tortoises. Discuss how tortoises are a kind of turtle. Read *Anansi Goes Fishing, The Flying Tortoise, Yertle the Turtle, Tortoise Brings the Mail* or *The Turtle and the Monkey* for fun.

Creative Writing

Think of different kinds of animals and attributes. (For example: kangaroo/jumping.) Come up with different contests the animals can have. Then write a sports page with headlines, articles and pictures for the contests. Young children can draw pictures or make up puppet shows for the contests.

Movement

List different kinds of movements: walking, running, skipping, hopping, etc. Have different contests for fun, use a stopwatch and create a chart of the children's times or mark different distances in yards and meters, then compare.

Art

Make turtle shell paperweights out of clay.

Geography

Read books about the Galapagos Islands such as *Nilo and the Tortoise* or *"Galapagos" Means "Tortoises."* Locate the islands on a map or globe. Look up Charles Darwin in a children's encyclopedia.

Books

Folktale Versions

Amin, Karima. *The Adventures of Brer Rabbit and Friends.* Family Learning, 1999. A retelling of some of the stories collected by Joel Chandler Harris including "Brer Rabbit Finds His Match" which tells of the race between Brer Rabbit and Brer Terrapin.

Jones, Carol. *The Hare and the Tortoise.* Houghton Mifflin, 1996. A tortoise and a hare have a race.

Lowell, Susan. *The Tortoise and the Jackrabbit.* Rising Moon, 1994. A tortoise and a jackrabbit have a race in the southwestern desert.

Miles, Betty. *The Tortoise and the Hare.* Simon & Schuster, 1998. A tortoise and a hare have a race.

Vozar, David. *M. C. Turtle and the Hip Hop Hare: A Nursery Rap.* Doubleday, 1995. A race between a turtle and a hare along city streets.

Ward, Helen. *The Hare and the Tortoise.* Millbrook Press, 1999. A tortoise and a hare have a race.

Related Reading

Arnosky, Jim. *All About Turtles.* Scholastic, 2000. Describes turtles.

Berger, Melvin. *Look Out for Turtles.* HarperCollins, 1992. Describes turtles.

Fowler, Allan. *Turtles Take Their Time.* Children's Press, 1992. A simple description of turtles.

Galdone, Paul. *The Turtle and the Monkey.* Clarion Books, 1983. Turtle tries to get Monkey's help with a banana tree, but Monkey is greedy.

Goodman, Susan E. *Claws, Coats, and Camouflage: The Way Animals Fit Into their World.* Millbrook Press, 2001. Describes how different animals adapt, fit in, stay safe, get food and make a new generation.

Heller, Ruth. *"Galapagos" Means "Tortoises."* Sierra Club Books for Children, 2000. Poems about animals found on the Galapagos Islands.

Kimmel, Eric A. *Anansi Goes Fishing.* Holiday House, 1992. Anansi tries to trick Turtle into catching fish for him, but Turtle outwits Anansi.

Lewin, Ted. *Nilo and the Tortoise.* Scholastic, 1999. A young boy is temporarily stranded alone on a Galapagos island.

Lillegard, Dee. *Tortoise Brings the Mail.* Dutton Children's Books, 1997. Crow, Rabbit and Fox try to prove they can deliver mail better than Tortoise.

Mollel, Tololwa M. *The Flying Tortoise: An Igbo Tail.* Clarion Books, 1994. Explains how Mbeku, the tortoise, gets a checkered shell.

Pinkney, Jerry. *Aesop's Fables.* SeaStar Books, 2000. A collection of almost 60 stories with morals.

Seuss, Dr. *Yertle the Turtle and Other Stories.* Random House, 1958. Yertle the Turtle King wants to sit high on many turtles' backs.

Zoehfeld, Kathleen Weidner. *What Lives in a Shell?* HarperCollins, 1994. Describes animals such as turtles, snails and crabs.

The Tortoise and the Hare Puppet Patterns

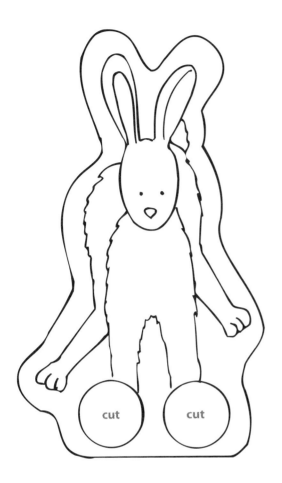
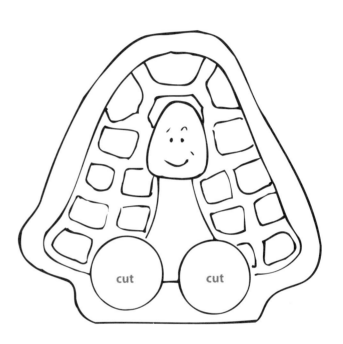

Materials:

- card stock
- scissors
- crayons or markers

Directions:

1. Photocopy the patterns. Enlarge if desired.
2. Color the patterns.
3. Cut and punch out the finger holes.

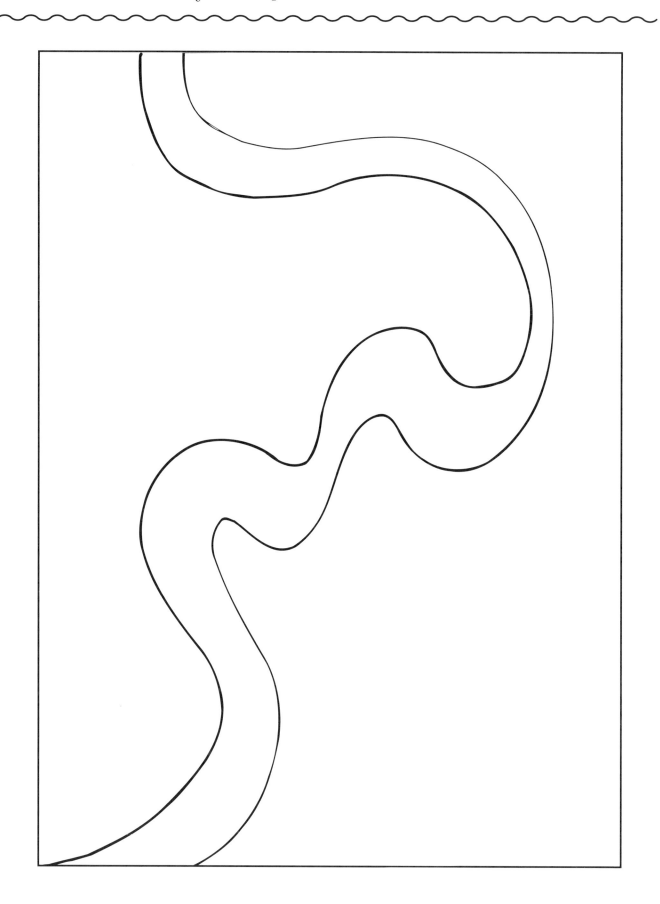

People

The Boy Who Cried Wolf

Programming Ideas

Theme: Learning from Stories

Setting the Scene

Explain that you are going to read *The Boy Who Cried Wolf*. Ask: Has anyone ever heard the story before? Can you tell the class what it is about? Explain that the story is one of Aesop's fables. A fable is a short story with a moral at the end. The moral of this story is that "no one believes a liar—even when he tells the truth."

Story

The Boy Who Cried "Wolf!" by Ellen Schecter

Read the book without using puppets. Immediately after reading it, put down the book and tell the story in your own words using the puppets (page 57).

Puppets

Have the puppets at a center or available to individual children when they finish their work. Students can practice telling the story using the puppets. Invite individuals to tell the story to the class.

Activities

Art

Cloud Pictures. Remind the children of the cloud pictures in *Hi, Clouds*. Collect several simple pictures (die-cut shapes, for example). Have the children paste cotton balls all over the picture. Post the "clouds" on a big blue bulletin board or on a wall. The children can guess what they are.

Bulletin Board

Title the board "And the Moral of the Story Is ..." Read several of Aesop's fables, then write the names of the fables on several sheets of paper and the morals on several sheets of paper. Illustrate both if possible and be sure to include *The Boy Who Cried Wolf*. Place the titles on one side of the board and the morals on the other. Have students tape string connecting the correct fable to the correct moral. When you need to fill some time, take the string down and have different students try matching the fables to the morals. Change the order of one side or the other.

Character Education

Ask: Did you learn anything from *The Boy Who Cried "Wolf!"*? What? Do you think you will be more likely to tell the truth based on what happened to the boy who lied? Discuss how the students will read and hear stories the rest of their lives. Some books can teach and help even when the author is just trying to entertain. Some of them teach so clearly that they put morals at the end of the story. These stories are called fables. Explain that Aesop, a man who lived long ago, wrote many fables. Read some fables and try to figure out the morals.

Game

Play "True or False." Version 1: Write statements based on your curriculum and ask the children to decide if your statement is true or false. Version 2: This game can be used for getting to know each other. For example: A child can state that he has two pets: a cat and a dog. True or false? Or a child can state that she was born in Florida. True or false? Once you get the true statement, find out how many others fit the statement (e.g., how many own pets; how many were born in Florida).

Math

Make your own counting chips using the picture of the sheep (page 58), enlarging or reducing as needed. Create chips out of laminated paper for the students to use or make a set for the overhead projector. Create math problems for the children to piece together at their desks. For example: The boy has nine sheep. Four go down the hill. How many are left? Write it on the board as a math problem. $9 - 4 = 5$. Continue doing this with addition or subtraction. Ask the children to come up and write the equations. Challenge them to make up math problems for each other.

Books

Folktale Versions

Littledale, Freya. *The Boy Who Cried Wolf.* Scholastic, 1975. A boy realizes the foolishness of telling lies.

Ross, Tony. *The Boy Who Cried Wolf.* Dial, 1985. A young boy gets in trouble from telling lies.

Schecter, Ellen. *The Boy Who Cried "Wolf!"* Gareth Stevens, 1997. A boy gets in trouble from telling lies.

Vozar, David. *Yo, Hungry Wolf! A Nursery Rap.* Random House, 1993. Contemporary retellings of three stories in rap.

Related Reading

Greene, Carol. *Hi, Clouds.* Children's Press, 1983. Two children see figures in the clouds.

Lynch, Tom. *Fables from Aesop.* Viking, 2000. Thirteen stories with morals.

Pinkney, Jerry. *Aesop's Fables.* SeaStar Books, 2000. A collection of almost 60 stories with morals.

The Boy Who Cried Wolf Puppet Patterns

Materials:

- tape
- scissors
- crayons, colored pencils or markers

Directions:

1. Photocopy the patterns. Adjust size if desired.

2. Color and cut out the patterns.

3. Tape the puppets to fit your finger.

townspeople

master

wolf

sheep

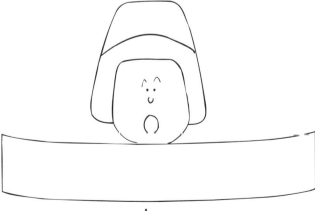

boy

Cinderella

Programming Ideas

Theme: Dreams

Setting the Scene

Explain that today's story contains things that are changed magically to make a person's dream come true. Challenge the students to name the story with this single clue: a pumpkin changes into a carriage.

Story

Cinderella by Barbara Karlin

Read the story. Discuss how the story has three important settings: inside Cinderella's house, the garden outside the house and the palace. Give each child a piece of paper for drawing one of the three backdrops to the story. Make sure you have a variety.

Puppets

Prepare one set of puppets on card stock: the two-sided puppets (Cinderella, the pumpkin, the mice, lizards and the rat) and the single-sided puppets (the prince, fairy godmother, stepmother and sisters) from pages 61–62. Collect three of the student-drawn backdrops made in the story activity. Ask for puppeteer volunteers. Read the story as the volunteers use the puppets and change the backdrops according to the action of the story. Read the story again as other students move the puppets and change the backdrops. Put the puppets and backdrops at a listening center for individual students to use.

Activities

Bulletin Board/Character Education

Title the board "Make Your Dreams Come True." Enlarge the picture of the fairy godmother puppet (page 62) to bulletin board size. Make several pumpkins (page 63). Have the students write, draw or cut out pictures of what they want to be when they grow up, places they want to go or other dreams they have.

These will be put on their pumpkins. Discuss some of the dreams and how staying in school, studying, reading, practicing, rehearsing and asking others to help you can help make those dreams come true. In short, discuss how if you work for your dreams, you can make them come true. Read *Amazing Grace, The Art Lesson, No Good In Art* or *The Wednesday Surprise.*

Creative Writing

Let each child make a puppet from the story (except for Cinderella). The child needs to make up a name for the puppet (even if it's the pumpkin) and tell what that puppet did before arriving in the Cinderella story and what happened to the puppet after the Cinderella story. (Older students can try writing the whole story from the puppet's perspective.)

Math (Graphing)

Read several of the Cinderella variations. List the titles across the top of a piece of poster board. Make many rectangles (more than your number of students). Ask each child which version they would most like to be in and then write the name of the student on a rectangle and tape it to the board under the title. Cover the titles and discuss how the bars formed by the rectangles indicate which titles are the most popular. Discuss why the students chose their versions.

Movement

Have your own "ball" by playing some music and letting the children dance. Perhaps the music or P.E. teachers can provide some music or dance instruction. (For a unit culmination, encourage the children to come dressed up, serve punch and cookies and crown everyone as Prince or Princess.)

Books

Folktale Versions

Cole, Babette. *Prince Cinders.* Putnam, 1987. Prince Cinders meets his princess.

Jackson, Ellen. *Cinder Edna.* Lothrop Lee & Shepard Books, 1994. Cinderella and Cinder Edna both have cruel stepmothers and stepsisters, but they have different approaches to their problems.

Jacobs, Joseph. *Tattercoats.* Putnam, 1989. A young girl is able to attend a royal ball with the help of a gooseherd.

Johnston, Tony. *Bigfoot Cinderrrrrella.* Putnam, 1998. A beary godfather enables Ella to attend a forest funfest and meet her prince.

Jungman, Ann. *Cinderella and the Hot Air Balloon.* Frances Lincoln, 1992. Cinderella has a party at her house.

Karlin, Barbara. *Cinderella.* Little, Brown and Company, 1989. A fairy godmother enables a girl to attend a ball and meet her prince.

Lowell, Susan. *Cindy Ellen: A Wild Western Cinderella.* Joanna Colter Books, 2000. A fairy godmother enables a girl to attend a rodeo and meet her prince.

Perlman, Janet. *Cinderella Penguin or, The Little Glass Flipper.* Scholastic, 1992. Cinderella the penguin attends a ball and meets her prince.

San Souci, Robert D. *Cendrillon: A Caribbean Cinderella Story.* Simon & Schuster, 1998. A young girl finds happiness with the help of her godmother.

San Souci, Robert D. *Sootface: An Ojibwa Cinderella Story.* Doubleday, 1994. An Indian woman finds happiness because of her kind and honest heart.

Related Reading

Bunting, Eve. *The Wednesday Surprise.* Clarion Books, 1989. A young girl teaches her grandmother to read.

Cohen, Miriam. *No Good In Art.* Dell, 1980. Jim learns that he is good in art after all.

De Paola, Tomie. *The Art Lesson.* Putnam, 1989. Tommy draws constantly because he wants to be an artist.

Hoffman, Mary. *Amazing Grace.* Scholastic, 1991. Grace discovers that she can do great things if she puts her mind to it.

Cinderella Puppet Directions

Two-sided Puppets

Materials:

- card stock
- popsicle sticks
- paper cups
- crayons or markers
- scissors
- tape or glue

Directions:

1. Photocopy the patterns on pages 61–62.
2. Color the patterns and cut them out.
3. Fold the patterns in half and tape or glue them to the popsicle stick.
4. Punch the stick through the bottom of the cup (see example).

Single-sided Puppets

- Same as above except paste the single puppet to the stick.

Cinderella Puppet Patterns

example

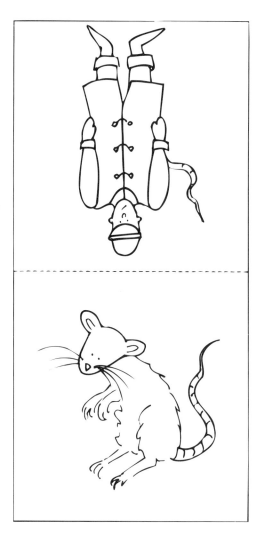

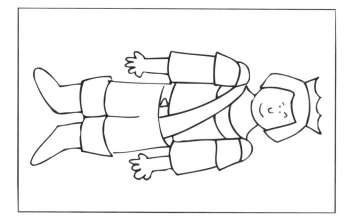

Pumpkin Patterns

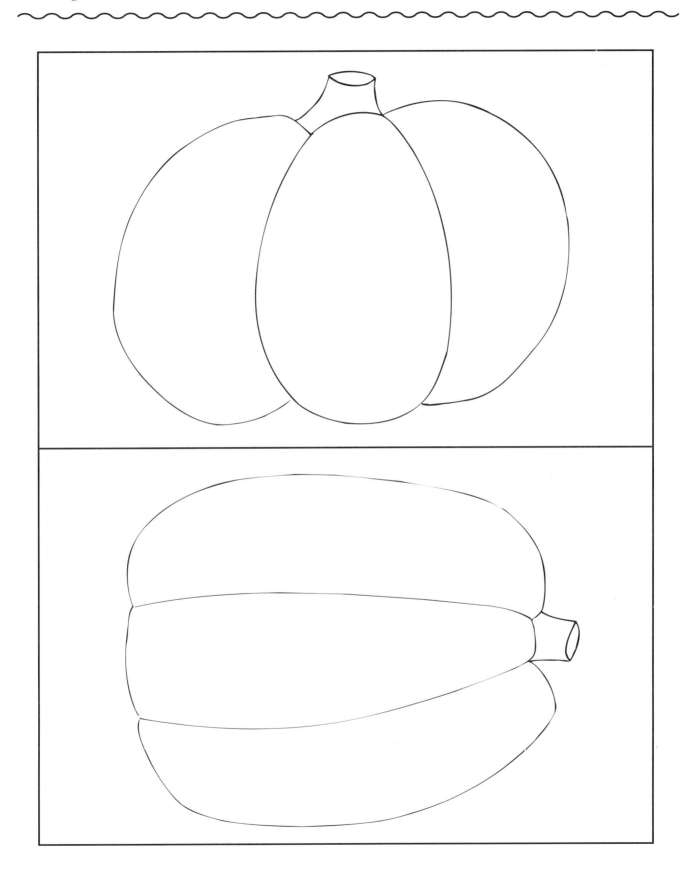

The Emperor's New Clothes

Programming Ideas

Theme: Believe in Yourself

Setting the Scene

Ask: Have you ever done something or said something and felt really foolish afterward? It's worse when someone sees you, isn't it? It would be worse if lots of people saw you, right? Explain that an emperor acts foolishly in the story you are about to read because he is afraid of what people think of him. In fact, many people act foolishly because they are afraid of what the others will think. Can anyone guess the name of the story?

Story

The Emperor's New Clothes by Demi

Read the story. At the end of the story, start a discussion by repeating the last sentence: "But he held his head high and continued to walk among his people." Was this a good thing for the emperor to do? What would you have done? Do you think the emperor and the others learned anything? If you do something foolish in the future, what should you do? (For example: laugh with others about yourself, apologize, keep from doing the foolish action again, etc.)

Puppets

Make puppets of the emperor on card stock, enlarging if desired (page 67). Smaller children may need help with cutting. Design clothes or use the pattern provided. Have a fashion show/parade of the emperor puppets in their "new" new clothes.

Activities

Art

Weave place mats from construction paper (page 66), then enjoy a "royal" snack.

Bulletin Board

Title the board "The Emperor's New Ideas." Enlarge the crown (page 67) and make several copies of it. Ask the children to list something the emperor learned in the story. Write each item on a crown and put it on the board. After reading other stories where the characters learn to believe in themselves, such as those in the related reading, list what those characters learned and add to the board.

Character Education

Discuss: Many times we do foolish things because we are afraid of what other people think, we are jealous of other people or we get mad at other people because we think they are laughing at us. People who aren't afraid of what other people think are called self-confident. That means they believe in themselves no matter what anyone else thinks. Sometimes it takes a long time to learn self-confidence. Then read about some characters who learn to believe in themselves. Read *The Biggest Nose, The Little Engine that Could, Strega Nona's Magic Lessons* or *The Very Worst Monster.*

Community Service

Collect coats and other clothes for a charitable organization.

Drama

Bring in a wide variety of clothes and accessories. Read *The Principal's New Clothes* or *Tacky and the Emperor.* Encourage the children to play dress-up and to create their own plays after they finish their work. If possible, take some photos and post.

Social Studies

Discuss how the United States has a president instead of an emperor and how the president is elected to lead the country for four years. Write a letter to the president thanking him or her for trying to make things better for all of us.

Books

Folktale Versions

Calmenson, Stephanie. *The Principal's New Clothes.* Scholastic, 1989. The familiar Hans Christian Andersen tale set in a public school.

Demi. *The Emperor's New Clothes: A Tale Set in China.* Margaret K. McElderry Books, 2000. The familiar Hans Christian Andersen tale set in old provincial China.

Lester, Helen. *Tacky and the Emperor.* Houghton Mifflin, 2000. Tacky the Penguin finds the emperor's clothes.

Westcott, Nadine Bernard. *The Emperor's New Clothes.* Little, Brown and Company, 1984. The familiar Hans Christian Andersen tale humorously illustrated.

Wheeler, Cindy. *The Emperor's Birthday Suit.* Random House, 1996. A beginning reader version of the familiar Hans Christian Andersen tale.

Related Reading

Caple, Kathy. *The Biggest Nose.* Houghton Mifflin, 1985. Eleanor is self-conscious of her nose.

De Paola, Tomie. *Strega Nona's Magic Lessons.* Harcourt, 1982. Big Anthony learns that he must be careful with magic.

Hutchins, Pat. *The Very Worst Monster.* Mulberry Books, 1985. Hazel Monster is jealous of her little brother.

Piper, Watty. *The Little Engine that Could.* Scholastic, 1930. The little engine proves that he can do it.

Place Mat Instructions

Materials:

- construction paper (2 different colors)
- scissors
- ruler
- pencil
- paste

Directions:

1. Fold a sheet of construction paper in half (square or rectangular).

2. Use a ruler to mark straight lines from the fold to 1" from the top. Cut on the lines. Be sure to stop 1" from the top.

3. Cut 1" strips from a second sheet of construction paper.

4. Weave the strips in and out of the first sheet to form a place mat.

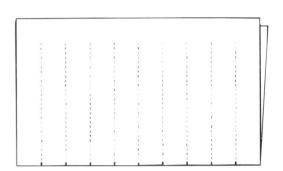

The Emperor's New Clothes Puppet Patterns

Materials:

- card stock
- crayons or markers
- scissors

Directions:

1. Photocopy the patterns. Enlarge them if desired.

2. Color the patterns and cut them out (do not cut the tabs off).

3. Fold the tabs around the puppet figure.

Crown Pattern

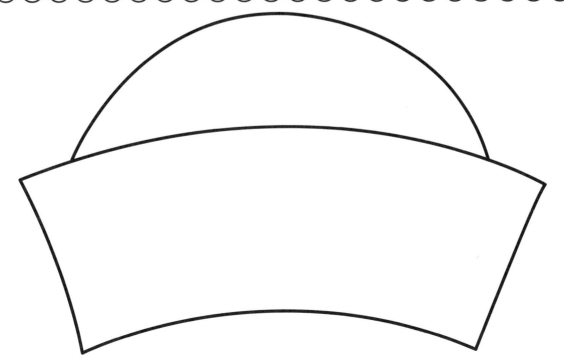

Hansel and Gretel

Programming Ideas

Theme: Teamwork

Setting the Scene

Before the class enters the room, hide the book *Hansel and Gretel* somewhere within the room. After the students enter, dim the lights and have them close their eyes. Walk about the room leaving stones (or counting chips) on a trail from the front of the room to where the book is hidden. Choose a student to follow the trail to find the book. When the student is at the book, ask the class if they can guess which story you are about to read.

Story

Hansel and Gretel by Rika Lesser

Pass out the backdrop pictures and finger puppets for the children to color as you read (pages 70–72). Each child will get three backdrop pictures (the woodcutter's cottage, the forest and the candy house) and five finger puppets (Hansel, Gretel, the father, the mother and the witch). Read the story.

Puppets

Talk about the different settings in the story. Discuss where the story begins and call that location Scene 1. Go through the story and list the settings. Each time the setting changes give it the appropriate scene number. List the scenes and settings on the board. Read the story again, this time announcing the scenes. The children can place the appropriate backdrop picture on their desks for each scene and use the finger puppets as you read the story.

Activities

Bulletin Board

Title the board "Teamwork." Brainstorm instances of teamwork and cooperation. Have the students draw examples and find pictures in magazines. Take pictures of the students working together and post them. **Extension Activity:** Come up with a team name for the class. (For example: Miss Nelson's class might have named themselves "Team Nelson.") Have a dress-up day where everyone wears similar clothes. Take pictures. You might have a service project the whole class can participate in.

Character Education

Discuss how Hansel and Gretel worked together throughout the story to help each other. They cooperated with each other. They worked as a team. Ask the children about sports activities. Discuss teamwork in that context. Then read *Miss Nelson Has a Field Day.* (If possible, read *Miss Nelson Is Missing!* prior to this discussion. It is the best introduction to the characters.) Discuss how the team played together and how the two sisters cooperated. Other stories to read include *Her Seven Brothers, The Five Chinese Brothers* and *The Seven Chinese Brothers.*

Cooking and Crafts

Make your own candy houses with graham crackers, frosting and gumdrops.

Game

Remind the students of how Hansel and Gretel worked together. Play a version of Hot and Cold. In this version, two students play while the rest of the students are the timekeepers. One of the students hides an object while the other isn't watching. Then, the student who hid the object has one minute to help his or her partner find the object using words like "hot," "cold," "warmer," etc. At the end of the minute, the object is revealed, if necessary, and that pair selects the next pair. **Note:** To make things trickier, try changing the object for each pair or don't let the seeker know what object he or she is looking for.

Music and Drama

Ask the music teacher for resources from the opera *Hansel and Gretel* by Engelbert Humperdinck. Perhaps the music teacher could teach some of the songs.

Books

Folktale Versions

Cole, Joanna (ed.). *Best-Loved Folktales of the World.* Doubleday, 1982. A collection of 200 folktales from around the world.

Grimm, Jakob, and Wilhelm Grimm. *Hansel and Gretel.* Dial, 1980. A brother and sister come to an edible house owned by a witch who likes to eat children.

Lesser, Rika. *Hansel and Gretel.* Putnam, 1984. A brother and sister come to an edible house owned by a witch who likes to eat children.

Marshall, James. *Hansel and Gretel.* Puffin, 1990. A brother and sister come to an edible house owned by a witch who likes to eat children.

Ray, Jane. *Hansel and Gretel.* Candlewick Press, 1997. A brother and sister come to an edible house owned by a witch who likes to eat children.

Thaler, Mike. *Hanzel and Pretzel.* Scholastic, 1997. A brother and sister come to an edible house owned by a witch who likes to eat children.

Related Reading

Allard, Harry. *Miss Nelson Has a Field Day.* Houghton Mifflin, 1985. A teacher helps a football team become winners.

Allard, Harry. *Miss Nelson Is Missing!* Houghton Mifflin, 1985. Students misbehave for a nice teacher and then learn good behavior from her replacement.

Bishop, Claire Huchet. *The Five Chinese Brothers.* Putnam, 1988. The classic children's book, first published in 1938, of how five brothers save each other because of their amazing abilities.

Goble, Paul. *Her Seven Brothers.* Bradbury Press, 1988. A Cheyenne legend on how the Big Dipper came to be.

Mahy, Margaret. *The Seven Chinese Brothers.* Scholastic, 1990. Seven brothers save each other because of their amazing abilities.

Hansel and Gretel Puppet Patterns

Materials:

- crayons or markers
- scissors
- tape

Directions:

1. Photocopy the patterns. Enlarge if desired.

2. Color the patterns and cut them out.

3. Adjust the band, then tape it together.

* Younger children may need help cutting.

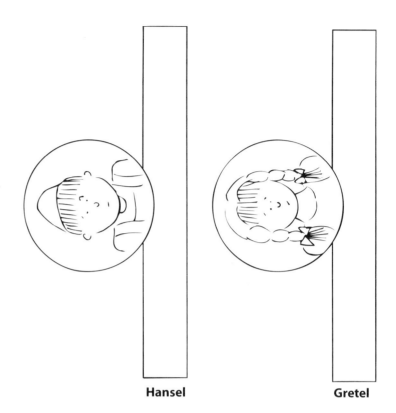

Hansel   **Gretel**

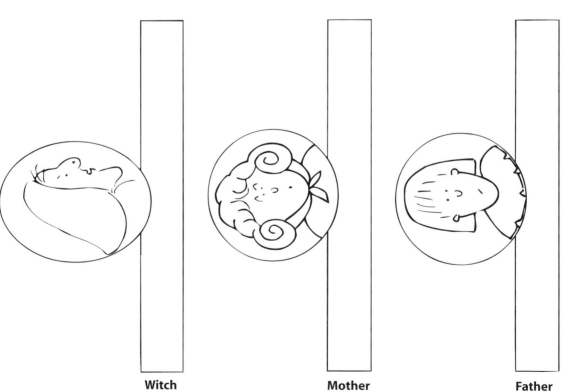

Witch   **Mother**   **Father**

Candy House

Jack and the Beanstalk

Programming Ideas

Theme: Trust

Setting the Scene

Have several students come to the front of the class. Ask another student to put them in order by height. Hand a Giant puppet (page 75) to that student to put in the line. Ask the class: Could you imagine being the size of this puppet? Would the puppet think we were giants?

Story

Jack and the Beanstalk by John Howe

Today you are going to hear a story about a boy who meets a giant. Can anyone guess the name of the story? Need a hint? *(Fee Fi Fo Fum!)*

Puppets

Make Jack and the Giant puppets (pages 75–78). Read the story again. Have students act out the story at their desktops. (Well-behaved classes could try sitting on the floor for the first part of the story and climbing up to the desktop for the castle section.)

Activities

Bulletin Boards

Title the board "Fee Fi Fo Fum." Enlarge the Castle in Clouds picture (page 79) and place it on a bulletin board or high on a wall. Post the students' puppets or their "Fee Fi Fo" verses. (Additional feature: Put a small house at floor level on the wall and make a vine with yarn or paper connecting the two.)

Character Education

Discuss Jack's actions. Was it okay to take those things from the giant? Why or why not? Read *Jim and the Beanstalk.* Compare the boys' actions. Which boy would you trust with your possessions or to help you when you are in trouble? Which would you most want as a friend? Is trust important for friends?

Game

Play the "Fee Fi Fo Fum" Game, a variation of "Simon Says." To play, the leader uses the phrase "Fee Fi Fo Fum" instead of "Simon Says."

Math

Hand out 10 counting chips to each child. In Cole's version of the folktale, as Jack is taking Milky-White (the cow) to the market, a man asks Jack if he knows how many beans make five. Jack replies, "Two in each hand and one in your mouth." Ask the children to put two in each hand and one on their heads. How many chips do they have? Try different combinations: five counting chips in one hand and two in another. How many is that? One on each shoulder and two in each hand. How many is that? etc.

Music

Make harps (page 78) and write new rhymes for the giant to sing or chant beginning with "Fee Fi Fo …" For example: "Fee Fe Fo Filly. Jack is being awfully silly. If he can beat me in a race, then I will make a silly face."

Science

Grow plants in cups and chart the growth.

Books

Folktale Versions

Briggs, Raymond. *Jim and the Beanstalk.* Coward-McCann, 1970. Jim climbs up a beanstalk and meets Jack's giant.

Cole, Joanna (ed.). *Best-Loved Folktales of the World.* Doubleday, 1982. A collection of 200 folktales from around the world.

Galdone, Paul. *Jack and the Beanstalk.* Clarion Books, 1974. A rhyming version of the story.

Howe, John. *Jack and the Beanstalk.* Little, Brown and Company, 1989. Jack climbs a beanstalk and outwits a giant.

Kellogg, Steven. *Jack and the Beanstalk.* Morrow Junior Books, 1991. Jack climbs a beanstalk and outwits an ogre.

Walker, Richard. *Jack and the Beanstalk.* Barefoot Books, 1999. Jack climbs a beanstalk and escapes a giant.

Wells, Rosemary. *Jack and the Beanstalk.* DK Publishing, 1997. Jack climbs a beanstalk and rescues his father from a giant.

Related Reading

Compton, Kenn, and Joanne Compton. *Jack the Giant Chaser: An Appalachian Tale.* Holiday House, 1993. Jack persuades a giant to leave Balsam Mountain for his own safety.

De Paola, Tomie. *Fin M'coul: The Giant of Knockmany Hill.* Holiday House, 1981. Fin and his wife outwit a bully.

Seeger, Pete. *Abiyoyo.* Aladdin Books, 2001. A boy and his father make a giant disappear.

Giant Puppet Instructions

Materials:

- construction paper
- scissors
- paste
- pencil
- markers or crayons
- paper lunch bags

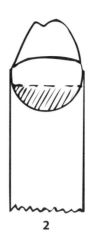

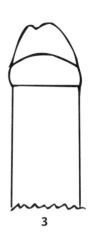

2   3

Directions:

1. Trace the pattern pieces from pages 76–77 onto construction paper and cut them out.

2. Paste the hat to the head.

3. Fold the face on the dotted line and paste the head to the bag, wrapping the fold under the bottom of the bag.

4. Paste the collar to the bag.

5. Paste the second face piece on the collar.

6. Add the sleeves and hands.

7. Draw the giant's features and hair.

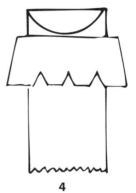

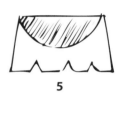

4   5

6/7

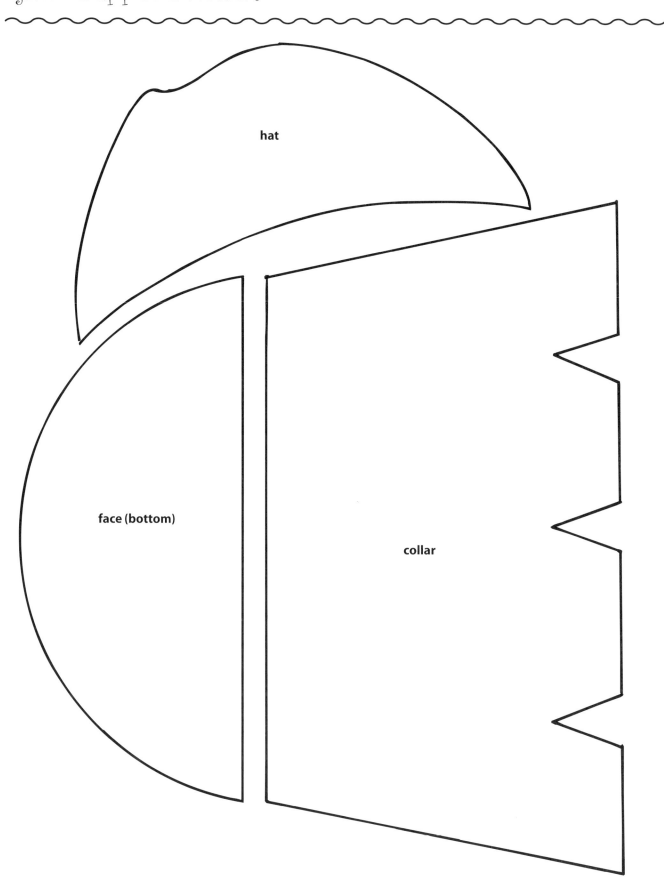

hat

face (bottom)

collar

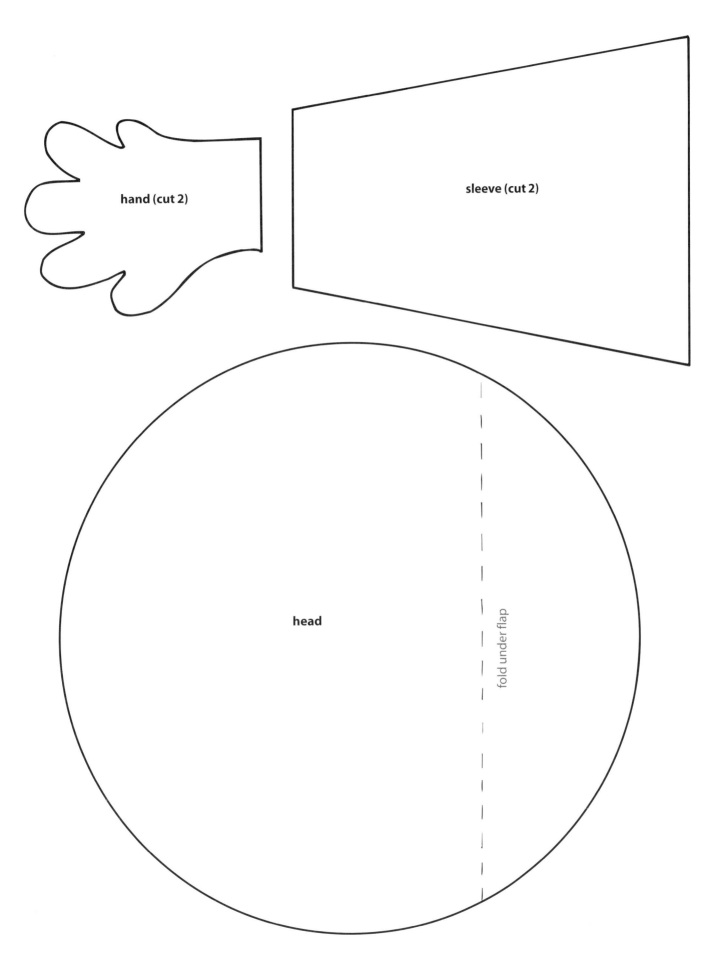

hand (cut 2)

sleeve (cut 2)

head

fold under flap

Jack and the Beanstalk Character Patterns

Materials:

- paper or card stock
- scissors
- tape or paste
- markers or crayons
- popsicle sticks

Directions:

1. Trace the pattern pieces.
2. Color and cut them out.
3. Tape the patterns to the sticks.

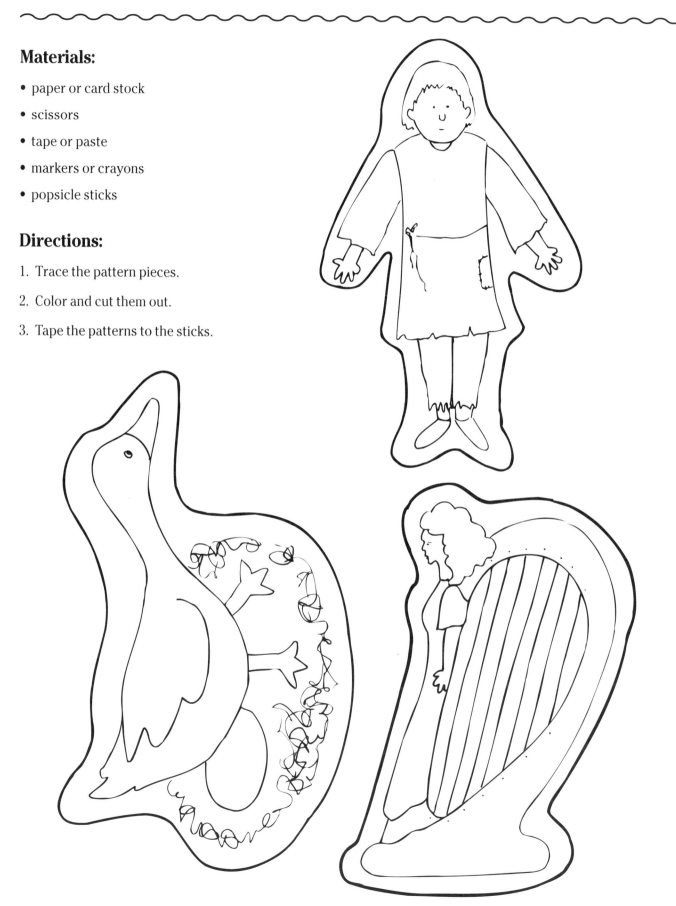

Castle in Clouds Pattern

The Legend of the Indian Paintbrush

Programming Ideas

Theme: Persistence

Setting the Scene

Ask: Did you know that every state has a state flower? What is our state flower? Explain that many flowers have legends about them. Wyoming's state flower is called the Indian Paintbrush. Today you are going to read a story about how the flower got its name.

Story

The Legend of the Indian Paintbrush by Tomie de Paola

Read the story straight through. Read the story again, looking particularly at Little Gopher's creations and the colors in the sky.

Puppets

Make Little Gopher puppets (page 81). Students can retell Little Gopher's story or give the puppet different names and create new stories. A cloud pattern is provided on page 82 for spirit guides if desired.

Activities

Art

Sculpt and decorate bowls (like Little Gopher's paint pots) or paint sunsets.

Bulletin Board

Cover the board with paper and entitle it "People With Persistence Accomplish Great Things." Explain that Little Gopher was faithful to his People and true to his gift. He never gave up even when he sometimes wanted to ride with the warriors. Another word for always trying and never giving up is "persistence." If you are persistent, you can accomplish great things in sports, career, school, helping others or the environment, etc.

Brainstorm things that the students might accomplish with persistence. Post the things they say, pictures cut from magazines and drawings (including Little Gopher) to create a big collage.

Character Education

Read *The Hare and the Tortoise.* Make a Venn diagram on the board. In one circle, list elements from *The Legend of the Indian Paintbrush* including how Little Gopher never gave up. In the other circle, list elements from *The Hare and the Tortoise* including how the tortoise never gave up. Ask what the two stories have in common and put the items in the shared part of the diagram (especially that they never gave up). Ask if the children learned anything from the story that can help them in their own lives.

Crafts

Make headbands with feathers. Discuss how animals and natural features (e.g., rivers) were often used in Native American names. Make up names and write them on the headbands.

Creative Writing

Make up stories about how the state flower or other local wildflowers got their names.

Research

Learn about different Native American tribes, particularly any that were in your area. Arrange for a guest speaker to come and talk to the class.

Books

Folktale Versions

De Paola, Tomie. *The Legend of the Indian Paintbrush.* Putnam, 1988. A young man is true to his artistic gifts and is able to bring the colors of the sunset down to the earth.

Related Reading

De Paola, Tomie. *The Legend of the Bluebonnet: An Old Tale of Texas.* Putnam, 1983. A young girl helps her people and brings the bluebonnet flower to Texas in this retelling of a Comanche legend.

Esbensen, Barbara. *The Star Maiden.* Little, Brown and Company, 1988. An Ojibwa legend of how water lilies came to the earth.

Goble, Paul. *Buffalo Woman.* Aladdin Books, 1984. A legend explaining the kinship felt between some tribes and the buffalo.

Goble, Paul. *The Gift of the Sacred Dog.* Aladdin Books, 1980. This legend explains how horses came to the Sioux tribe.

Goble, Paul. *Her Seven Brothers.* Bradbury Press, 1988. A Cheyenne legend on how the Big Dipper came to be.

Goble, Paul. *Love Flute.* Bradbury Press, 1988. A version of how the love flute came to be.

Ward, Helen. *The Hare and the Tortoise: A Fable from Aesop.* Millbrook, 1999. A hare is overconfident and loses a race.

Little Gopher Puppet Pattern

Materials:

- scissors
- tape
- markers or crayons

Directions:

1. Photocopy the patterns.

2. Color and cut them out.

3. Tape the puppets to your finger.

Cloud Pattern

The Pied Piper of Hamelin

Programming Ideas

Theme: Keeping Promises

Setting the Scene

Play a few notes on a recorder* or flute. Explain that you are about to read a story about a piper—a musician who plays a similar instrument to the one you are playing. Ask if anyone knows the name of the story or what the story is about.

* Most music teachers and music stores have inexpensive recorders available.

Story

The Pied Piper of Hamelin by Deborah Hautzig

Make a story cube or individual puppets (pages 85–86). Read the story to the class. Read the story again (or tell the story in your own words) simultaneously turning your story cube or using the puppets to match the action of the story.

Puppets

Have the children make their own story cubes or individual puppets. Tell the story to each other in pairs or small groups.

Activities

Bulletin Board

Title the board "I Want to Do Well in School—So I Promise I Will Try To ..." After putting the title on the board, ask the children if they know why you worded it this way instead of simply "I Promise I Will ..." Discuss how sometimes it is impossible to keep a promise and how you should not make promises if you know you cannot keep them. Then ask the students to think of things they can do which will help them do well in school. If a student can promise to try something, write it down and post it on the board.

Character Education

Ask: Do you believe it is important to keep your promises? Why? What happens if you don't keep your promises? What if you say you will do something but you don't say "I Promise"? Is it important to keep your word even if you don't say "I Promise?" Read stories like *A Promise Is a Promise, Strega Nona, The Boy Who Cried "Wolf!," Little Red Riding Hood* or *Heckedy Peg* and discuss the importance of keeping promises and keeping your word.

Movement

Select a student to be the Piper. Play some music, preferably instrumental. While the music is playing, the Piper walks or skips around the room until you or a student randomly pauses the music. The person the Piper stops next to shakes the Piper's hands and then follows the Piper in a parade. Keep going until every student is following in the parade.

Optional: Make up a rhythmic hand-clap pattern (or have the students make up a pattern) to a rhyme like "You're the Pied Piper. I've heard of you. Here is the money we promised to you."

Music

Ask the music teacher for resources that demonstrate different kinds of musical instruments or use Prokofiev's *Peter and the Wolf,* a popular musical composition that teaches some of the instruments.

Science

Use the story as the starting point for a lesson on sound. Explain that sound is produced by vibrations or waves of air that travel from the source of the sound to our ears. Show the effects of sound vibrations by making a drum. Cover a cake tin with a circle cut from a balloon and secure it with a rubber band. Place sugar on the drum. Hit a baking tray with a wooden spoon near the drum. The sugar will move from the sound vibrations. Holding the tray at different distances will make the sugar move differently.

Books

Folktale Versions

Adler, Naomi. *Play Me A Story: Nine Tales About Musical Instruments.* Millbrook Press, 1998. A collection of nine musical tales from all over the world including "The Pied Piper of Hamelin," a tale from Germany.

Cole, Joanna (ed.). *Best-Loved Folktales of the World.* Doubleday, 1982. A collection of 200 folktales from around the world.

Hautzig, Deborah. *The Pied Piper of Hamelin.* Random House, 1989. A town pays a terrible price for failing to keep a promise.

Holden, Robert. *The Pied Piper of Hamelin.* Houghton Mifflin, 1997. A town pays a terrible price for failing to keep a promise.

Mayer, Mercer. *The Pied Piper of Hamelin.* Macmillan, 1987. A town pays a terrible price for failing to keep a promise.

Related Reading

De Paola, Tomie. *Strega Nona.* Prentice-Hall, 1975. Big Anthony has trouble with Strega Nona's magic pasta pot.

Hyman, Trina Schart. *Little Red Riding Hood.* Holiday House, 1983. A girl encounters a dangerous wolf.

Munsch, Robert, and Michael Kusugak. *A Promise Is a Promise.* Annick Press, 1988. A young girl breaks her promise and fishes on the sea ice.

Schecter, Ellen. *The Boy Who Cried "Wolf!"* Bantam Books, 1994. A boy gets in trouble from telling lies.

Wood, Audrey. *Heckedy Peg.* Harcourt, 1992. A mother must save her children from a witch.

The Pied Piper of Hamelin Cube Pictures

Materials:

- paper or card stock
- crayons or markers
- scissors
- popsicle sticks
- tape or paste

Directions:

1. Photocopy the puppets and enlarge if desired.

2. Color and cut out the puppets.

3. Tape sticks to the back of each puppet.

Story Cube Pattern

Materials:

- paper or card stock
- scissors
- crayons or markers
- paste

Directions:

1. Photocopy the box and pictures. (Create a master by pasting the pictures on the box and copying.)

2. Color and cut the patterns.

3. Fold the tabs to form a cube. Tape.

Red Riding Hood

Programming Ideas

Theme: Good Manners

Setting the Scene

Ask: What might you say if I comment, "My, what big eyes you have." (Hopefully one answer will be "The better to see you with, my dear!") What might you say if I comment, "My, what big ears you have." What might you say if I comment, "My, what big teeth you have!" Who can name the story we are about to read?

Story

Little Red Riding Hood by Trina Schart Hyman

Read the story. Ask the children to sequence the story. (For example: The story starts at Red Riding Hood's house. Then Red follows the path through the woods. Meets the wolf. Picks some flowers, etc.) Read the book again or read a similar version such as James Marshall's.

Puppets

Copy the finger puppets (page 89) onto card stock. Younger children may need help with cutting. Read the story again and have them reenact the story at their desks. One side of the desk can be mother's house, the other can be grandmother's house and the woods are in between.

Activities

Bulletin Board

Title the board "Good Manners Are Like Flowers—They Make the World More Beautiful." Make flowers (page 90) and then list a good manner, word or phrase on each one. For example: "Please," "Thank You," "Good Morning." Post on the board.

Character Education

Ask: What are good manners? Do you think good manners are important? Why or why not? Explain that you and most people think good manners are very important. Read *What Do You Say, Dear?* or *Perfect Pigs* and discuss good manners.

Following Directions

Write down directions for the children to follow. The directions should take them many places through the school and finally outdoors where they can have some goodies. The directions can be straightforward or simple riddles. Perhaps carry a basket and tell the children that they need to find grandmother's house. Read one of the Red Riding Hood variations while eating the treats.

Game

Have the children stand up at their seats. The first person says the following statement and fills in the blank with a noun beginning with the letter A: "I went to grandmother's house. She has _____ (apples, aardvarks, an airplane, etc.)." The second person says "I went to grandmother's house. She has a(pples) and _____ (books, bananas, etc.)." When students can't remember the sequence or can't come up with words, they sit down. With younger students, hold up letters in the alphabet and help them with the sequence.

Safety

Red Riding Hood made some poor choices when she spoke to a stranger. Have the class list some safety tips. After they list as many as they can, read *Safety Around Strangers* and try to list more.

Books

Folktale Versions

Artell, Mike. *Petite Rouge: A Cajun Red Riding Hood.* Dial, 2001. A young duck outwits a crocodile with the help of a cat.

De Regniers, Beatrice Schenk. *Red Riding Hood.* Aladdin Books, 1972. A girl encounters a dangerous wolf. The story is told in verse.

Emberley, Michael. *Ruby.* Little, Brown and Company, 1990. A tough little city mouse forgets her mother's advice about talking to strangers on the way to her grandmother's house.

Ernst, Lisa Campbell. *Little Red Riding Hood: A Newfangled Prairie Tale.* Aladdin, 1995. A wolf deals with both a little and a big Red Riding Hood as he tries to steal some muffins.

Hyman, Trina Schart. *Little Red Riding Hood.* Holiday House, 1983. A girl encounters a dangerous wolf.

Marshall, James. *Red Riding Hood.* Puffin Books, 1987. A girl encounters a dangerous wolf.

Young, Ed. *Lon Po Po: A Red-Riding Hood Story from China.* Scholastic, 1989. Three children encounter a dangerous wolf while their mother is at their grandmother's house.

Related Reading

Brown, Marc, and Stephen Krensky. *Perfect Pigs: An Introduction to Manners.* Little, Brown and Company, 1983. Pigs demonstrate good manners with family, going to parties, with friends, in public places, etc.

Joslin, Sesyle. *What Do You Say, Dear?* HarperCollins, 1958. Shows good manners can occur even in humorous settings.

Raatma, Lucia. *Safety Around Strangers.* Bridgestone Books, 1999. Provides safety tips including staying with groups, safe routes and family code words.

Red Riding Hood Finger Puppet Patterns

Materials:

- paper or card stock
- scissors
- crayons, colored pencils or markers
- tape

Directions:

1. Photocopy the puppets.
2. Color and cut out the puppets.
3. Tape the puppets to your fingers.

Red Riding Hood

Mother

Grandma

Woodsman

Wolf

Daisy

center (cut 1)

petals (cut 6)

Iris

petals (cut 3)

bottom (cut 1)

Rumpelstiltskin

Programming Ideas

Theme: Using Our Gifts

Setting the Scene

Ask the students to think of cartoons, books and movies where the people have magical powers. Ask: What are some of their magical powers? If you could have one magical power, what would you choose?"

Story

Rumpelstiltskin by Paul Galdone

Explain that you are going to read a story where a character has a magical power—the power to spin straw into gold. Ask if anyone knows the name of the story.

Puppets

Read the story once. Read the story again, but as you read, place the silhouettes (page 93) on the overhead projector when the appropriate word occurs in the story. Have the children say the word. (**Note:** Put the girl silhouette up when the word "daughter" or "girl" appears in the story and use the same word or phrase every time, such as "miller's daughter.") Afterward, give the children a puppet of the miller's daughter or Rumpelstiltskin (page 94) to color, enlarging if desired.

Activities

Art—Yarn Art

Explain that spinning wheels are normally used to spin wool into yarn. Make an art table or center. Put flat containers with different colors of paint, lengths of yarn and blank paper on the table. The children take a string and wiggle it across the page or fold the paper in half over the string and pull the string out to create a picture. Read *Mouse Paint* for a follow-up story on colors, and *Charlie Needs a Cloak* or *Farmer Brown Shears his Sheep* for a follow-up story on yarn.

Bulletin Board

Title the board "We All Have Special Gifts." Make copies of the gift (page 95), enlarging if necessary. Write each student's name on one. Interview each child and ask him or her to name two abilities or qualities that he or she has. Then assign homework (perhaps with a note home) asking the adults in the student's life to list some of the special abilities or qualities they have observed in the student. Add these words to the pictures and post on the bulletin board. If pictures are available, attach the children's pictures to the gift.

Character Education

Ask the children if they can name some of their gifts (abilities/qualities). Explain that we all are special—even when we do not think so. Read *Fritz and the Beautiful Horses* or *Katie Couldn't.*

Game

Play "I Spy Someone Wearing ... (Yellow)" or "I Spy Someone Whose Name Begins With ... (R)." This game reinforces alphabet or color recognition and provides a positive way for children to be noticed by their peers.

Language Arts—Alphabet Book

Explain that "Rumpelstiltskin" was the only name used in the book. It begins with the letter R. Challenge the class to come up with a name for every letter in the alphabet. Then think of a corresponding ability or characteristic. For example: Alfred can fly an airplane. Betty is brave. Write each one at the bottom of a page. Then create a classroom book by passing out the pages and having each child draw a person.

Books

Folktale Versions

Galdone, Paul. *Rumpelstiltskin.* Houghton Mifflin, 1985. A magical little man saves a miller's daughter by spinning straw into gold.

Gay, Marie-Louise. *Rumpelstiltskin.* Groundwood Books, 1997. A magical little man saves a miller's daughter by spinning straw into gold.

Hamilton, Virginia. *The Girl Who Spun Gold.* Blue Sky Press, 2000. A West Indian variant of the story of a little man who saves a woman by spinning straw into gold.

Stanley, Diane. *Rumpelstiltskin's Daughter.* Morrow Junior Books, 1997. A twist on the old tale with a happy ending for all.

Related Reading

Brett, Jan. *Fritz and the Beautiful Horses.* Houghton Mifflin, 1981. Fritz the pony rescues some children.

De Paola, Tomie. *Charlie Needs a Cloak.* Simon & Schuster, 1973. A shepherd makes a red cloak using his sheep's wool.

McDaniel, Becky Bring. *Katie Couldn't.* Scholastic Library Publishing, 1985. Katie feels she cannot do anything.

Sloat, Teri. *Farmer Brown Shears his Sheep.* DK Publishing, 2000. Farmer Brown's sheep are cold after shearing.

Walsh, Ellen S. *Mouse Paint.* Harcourt, 1989. Three mice explore paint.

Rumpelstiltskin Silhouette Patterns

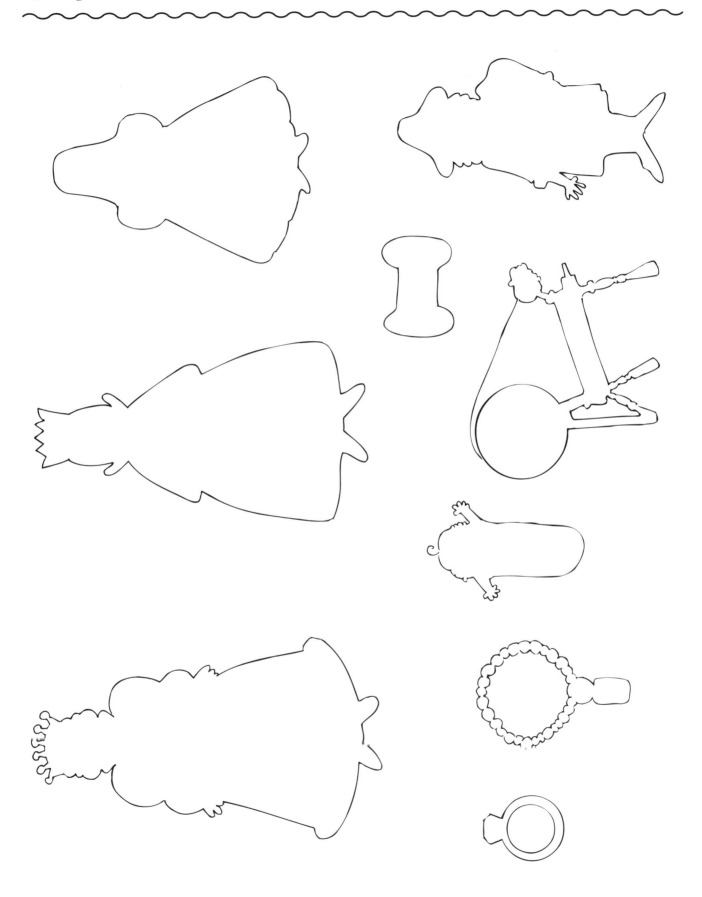

Rumpelstiltskin and Daughter Puppet Patterns

Gift Pattern

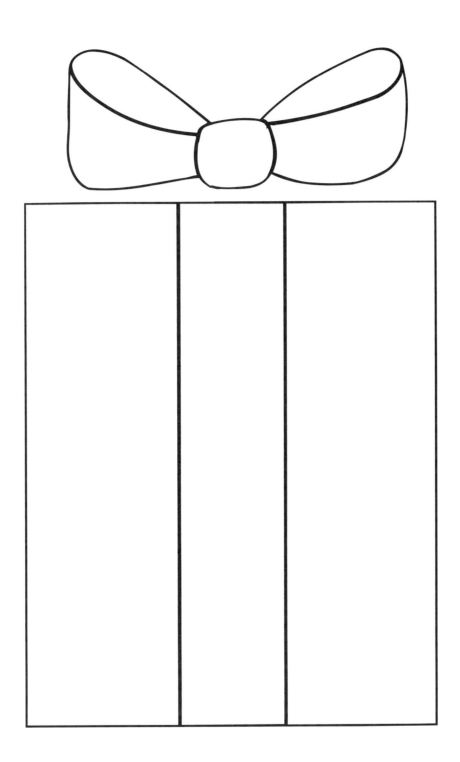

The Teeny Tiny Woman

Programming Ideas

Theme: Bravery

Setting the Scene

Ask: Have you ever felt like you were tiny compared to the adults around you? Have you ever felt like you were teeny-tiny? Explain that the story is about a teeny-tiny woman who has a teeny-tiny adventure.

Story

The Teeny-Tiny Woman by Paul Galdone

Read the book once. On the second reading, encourage the children to do the ghostly voice with you. Read other stories about tiny people or animals such as *George Shrinks, Thumbelina, Tom Thumb, The Teeny Tiny Teacher* and *Two Bad Ants.* Look at some photos from *Look Book* or a similar book, try to guess what they are and discuss how a change in size would change how ordinary things appear.

Puppets

Copy the puppet of the Teeny-Tiny woman (page 97) onto card stock. Have volunteers cut them out for the children—especially the holes for the fingers. Hand out the "maps" of the teeny-tiny woman's walk (page 98) or large sheets of paper on which the children can draw their own maps. Children can color and add features such as bushes, funny gravestones, etc. Read the story while the puppets follow the action of the story on the maps.

Activities

Bulletin Board

Title the board "Teeny Tiny Adventures." Have each child either write a prompt,* draw a picture or design a comic strip featuring a tiny person or animal dealing with the large world. Read adventures of other tiny characters.

*A prompt might be: When I woke up this morning, I was the size of _____.

Character Education (Bravery)

Discuss being afraid like the teeny-tiny woman. Ask if she was being a teeny-tiny bit brave when she peeked out from the covers to say, "Take it!" Discuss how being brave means doing what you need to do even when you are afraid. Read *"I Am Not Afraid," There's a Nightmare In My Closet* or *There's Something In My Attic.*

Craft

Make a "Favorite Story Quilt." Cut many construction paper squares of different colors—one for each student. Each student chooses a favorite children's story and draws a scene or writes the title and decorates it. Assemble the squares and display. Bring in a real quilt or ask a guest speaker to discuss quilting. Read *Sam Johnson and the Blue Ribbon Quilt.*

Creative Writing

Do you find the story a little bit spooky? Do you like spooky stories? Read *A Dark Dark Tale* or *In a Dark Dark Room.* As a class, make up a similar story.

Observation Walk

Go on a walk around the school campus. Observe what you see so you can make a list when you return to the classroom. If you have different kinds of trees nearby, try to collect a leaf from each different kind to identify. Read *The Teeny Tiny Teacher.*

Books

Folktale Versions

Calmenson, Stephanie. *The Teeny Tiny Teacher.* Scholastic, 1998. A teacher and her class are frightened after picking up a teeny-tiny bone for their science lesson.

Cole, Joanna (ed.). *Best-Loved Folktales of the World.* Doubleday, 1982. A collection of 200 folktales from around the world.

Galdone, Paul. *The Teeny-Tiny Woman.* Clarion Books, 1984. A woman is frightened after picking up a teeny-tiny bone.

O'Connor, Jane. *The Teeny Tiny Woman.* Random House, 1986. A woman is frightened after picking up a teeny-tiny bone.

Winters, Kay. *The Teeny Tiny Ghost.* HarperCollins, 1997. A tiny ghost is frightened on Halloween.

Related Reading

Andersen, Hans Christian. *Thumbelina.* Doubleday, 1991. A tiny girl has many adventures.

Brown, Ruth. *A Dark Dark Tale.* Dial, 1981. A surprise ending awaits at the end of a dark, dark story.

Ernst, Lisa Campbell. *Sam Johnson and the Blue Ribbon Quilt.* Mulberry, 1983. The men and women of the Rosedale quilting clubs collaborate on a winning quilt.

French, Fiona. *Little Inchkin.* Dial, 1994. A tiny young man becomes a Samurai swordsman.

Hoban, Tana. *Look Book.* Greenwillow Books, 1997. Guess everyday objects from looking at a small part of the whole.

Joyce, William. *George Shrinks.* HarperCollins, 1985. A young boy's adventures when he wakes up the size of a mouse.

Mann, Kenny. *"I Am Not Afraid!"* Byron Press, 1993. A young Masai boy learns bravery from his older brother.

Mayer, Mercer. *There's a Nightmare In My Closet.* Dial, 1968. A young boy faces his fears.

Mayer, Mercer. *There's Something In My Attic.* Dial, 1988. A young girl faces her fears.

Schwartz, Alvin. *In a Dark, Dark Room, and Other Scary Stories.* Harper & Row, 1984. Seven scary stories based on traditional folktales.

Van Allsburg, Chris. *Two Bad Ants.* Houghton Mifflin, 1988. Two ants have an adventure.

Watson, Richard Jesse. *Tom Thumb.* Harcourt, 1989. A tiny boy survives many perilous adventures to become the smallest Knight of the Round Table.

The Teeny Tiny Woman Puppet Pattern

Materials:

- card stock
- scissors
- crayons
- hole punch

Directions:

1. Photocopy the puppets. Enlarge them if desired.

2. Color and cut out the puppets.

3. Punch out the finger holes.

Tip: Make a master of 12 puppets on a page.

The Teeny Tiny Woman Map

Places

Baba Yaga

Programming Ideas

Theme: Forests

Setting the Scene

Say: I am thinking of a certain kind of place. Let's see if you can guess it with these clues. Part of the "Hansel and Gretel" story takes place here. Part of "Red Riding Hood" does, too. Snow White runs into this place before the seven dwarves find her. What is this place? (*A forest.*)

Story

Bony-Legs by Joanna Cole

Explain that a forest is a large area covered with so many trees that the area is shaded. The story you are about to read takes place in a forest in Russia. Locate Russia on a map. Read *Bony-Legs*. Explain that the character of Bony-Legs is based on a scary witch from Russian folktales called Baba Yaga. Read another version of the story if possible.

Puppets

Make the Bony-Leg house and puppet (pages 103–104). Read the story again. Every time Bony-Legs is mentioned, the children can move the puppet up so it is seen.

Activities

Community Service

Discuss Sasha's kindness to the dog and the cat in *Bony-Legs* and ask about pets the children have. Collect money to give to the Humane Society.

Folklore

Ask the children to list as many fairy tales and stories as they can. Go through the titles and decide which take place, at least in part, in forests. Read some of the stories listed or try *Flossie and the Fox, Rainbow Crow* or *The Banza.*

Geography

Read *The Forests* to learn more about forests. Collect leaves of trees in the area and identify them. Try making a simple nature journal by observing and drawing a natural area near the school over the course of a week (or longer).

Music

Play Modest Mussorgsky's "Hut on Hen's Legs" from his composition *Pictures at an Exhibition.* Listen to the whole work as the children draw a scene from one of the Baba Yaga stories.

Science

Discuss the types of natural areas near the school. Are forests nearby? Lead the discussion toward a backyard science experiment or activity from books such as *Backyard* or *Science Wizardry for Kids.*

Books

Folktale Versions

Cole, Joanna (ed.). *Best-Loved Folktales of the World.* Doubleday, 1982. A collection of 200 folktales from around the world.

Cole, Joanna. *Bony-Legs.* Scholastic, 1983. A girl survives a visit with Bony-Legs because of her kindness to others.

Johnston, Tony. *Alice Nizzy Nazzy: The Witch of Santa Fe.* Putnam, 1995. Manuela must visit a witch's house to get her sheep.

Kimmel, Eric A. *Baba Yaga: A Russian Folktale.* Holiday House, 1991. A girl survives a visit with Baba Yaga because of her kindness to others.

Mayer, Marianna. *Baba Yaga and Vasilisa the Brave.* Morrow Junior Books, 1994. A girl and her doll escape from the dangerous Baba Yaga.

McCaughrean, Geraldine. *Grandma Chickenlegs.* Carolrhoda Books, 2000. A girl and her doll escape from the dangerous Grandma Chickenlegs.

Oram, Hiawyn. *Baba Yaga and the Wise Doll.* Dutton Children's Books, 1997. A girl and her doll escape from the dangerous Baba Yaga.

Polacco, Patricia. *Babushka Baba Yaga.* Philomel Books, 1993. The legendary Baba Yaga disguises herself and becomes a babushka.

Related Reading

Higginson, Mel. *The Forests.* Rourke, 1994. An overview of forests.

Kenda, Margaret, and Phyllis S. Williams. *Science Wizardry For Kids.* Scholastic, 1992. Over 200 inexpensive scientific experiments that children can perform.

Leslie, Clare Walker, and Charles E. Roth. *Keeping a Nature Journal—Discover a Whole New Way of Seeing the World Around You.* Storey Books, 2000. A guide to getting started journaling with a section on journaling with school groups.

McKissack, Patricia C. *Flossie and the Fox.* Dial, 1986. A little girl insists that a fox prove he is a fox before she will be frightened.

Silver, Donald M. *Backyard.* W. H. Freeman and Company, 1993. A look at common plants and animals.

Van Laan, Nancy. *Rainbow Crow.* Dragonfly Books, 1989. Crow saves the forest animals from the cold by getting fire from the Sky Spirit.

Wolkstein, Diane. *The Banza: A Haitian Story.* Puffin, 1984. A goat receives a gift from the tiger that became her friend.

Bony-Leg House Instructions

Materials:

- construction paper or colored paper (brown or tan)
- scissors
- pipe cleaners (yellow or orange)
- tape
- paste
- Styrofoam cups
- straws or unsharpened pencils

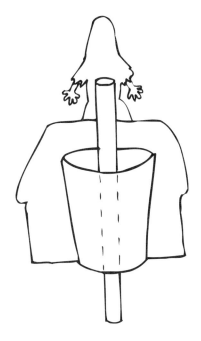

Directions:

1. Photocopy the house pattern on colored paper or have the students color a white copy. Cut the house out.

2. Carefully punch a hole in the bottom center of the cup with a pencil.

3. Paste the house to the cup as shown.

4. Color Bony-leg and cut out.

5. Tape Bony-leg to a straw or pencil top.

6. Place the straw or pencil in the cup and raise the puppet up and down.

7. Take a pipe cleaner and cut two 4" pieces and two 1½" pieces for the house legs.

8. Tape the longer pieces to the house as shown and twist the smaller pieces to form legs.

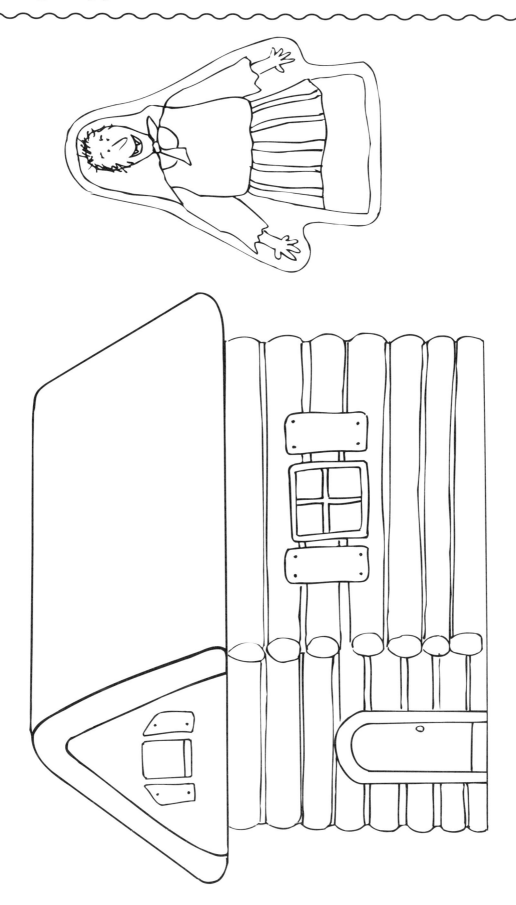

Coyote Steals the Blanket

Programming Ideas

Theme: Deserts

Setting the Scene

Ask: Have you ever known anyone to do the opposite of what they are told? Explain that this story features Coyote—a trickster used in many North American Indian tales who can be foolish or clever, helpful or harmful.

Story

Coyote Steals the Blanket by Janet Stevens

Ask the children to look at the cover of the book. What is the setting? (Prompt if necessary: Is it forest? swamp? ocean?) Explain that the setting is the desert—but not like the Sahara desert. The title states that this is an Ute tale. The state of Utah is named for the Ute Indians. Locate Utah on a map. Explain that it is a mountain-desert state. Compare Utah to the state where you are. Read the story.

Puppets

Get a blanket or afghan and prepare the coyote hat and a set of puppets (pages 107–109) prior to the activity. **Note:** Optional hats for all characters are provided (page 108). After reading the story one or more times, explain to the students that they are going to act out the story using their own words. Ask for a volunteer to act out Coyote and three other volunteers to be puppeteers (or act out the other characters). Drape the blanket over the back of a chair placed in the front of the room to denote the boulder. Then have the Coyote actor begin improvising. The rest of the students will provide the "Rumble, rumble, rumble" lines. If improvising is too difficult at first, the students can act out the story as you read aloud.

Activities

Art

Read *The Magic Weaver of Rugs* or look at *Songs From the Loom* and design your own blankets.

Geography

1. Make a KWL chart on an overhead transparency or on chart paper.

2. Ask the children to brainstorm everything they Know (or think they know) about deserts. List these in the K column. Then ask them What they want to learn about deserts. List the questions in the W column. (Possible questions: What is a desert? How can I tell desert areas on a map or globe? What is the biggest desert in the world? What are the names of deserts in the United States? What animals live in deserts? Can people live in deserts?)

3. Explain that over the next few days you are all going to research the answers to those questions, add interesting information to the L (for what they Learn) column and see if the list in the K column is correct.

4. Ask the children to ask their families at home for answers to the questions, look up deserts in a children's encyclopedia and/or read *Deserts*.

5. Fill in the L column as a class.

K	W	L

Games

Ask if anyone has ever played marbles. Games with marbles have existed a long time. Marbles can be stone, clay, wood, glass, steel, etc. Bring in marbles or make your own from clay. Play some games.

Folklore

Read other Coyote trickster tales. Try making up a new one. (Possible story starter: Explain why coyotes howl at night.)

Science

Read *The Big Rock* and discuss. Ask students to bring in at least one rock to show the class. Create a class rock collection and store it in a display box.

Books

Folktale Versions

Robinson, Gail, and Douglas Hill. *Coyote the Trickster: Legends of the North American Indians.* Crane Russak, 1976. Twelve stories featuring Coyote, the trickster.

Stevens, Janet. *Coyote Steals the Blanket: A Ute Tale.* Holiday House, 1993. Coyote is in trouble after taking a blanket that does not belong to him.

Related Reading

Aardema, Verna. *Borreguita and the Coyote.* Knopf, 1991. A little lamb outwits a coyote.

Cole, Joanna, and Stephanie Calmenson. *Marbles: 101 Ways To Play.* Morrow Junior Books, 1998. Marble games and activities.

Goldin, Barbara Diamond. *Coyote and the Fire Stick: A Pacific Northwest Indian Tale.* Gulliver Books, 1996. Coyote helps the People get Fire.

Hiscock, Bruce. *The Big Rock.* Aladdin, 1988. Explains how a rock in the Adirondacks came to be there.

Lowell, Susan. *The Three Little Javelinas.* Northland Publishing, 1992. A version of "The Three Little Pigs" with javelinas and a coyote.

Lye, Keith. *Rocks and Minerals.* Raintree Steck-Vaughn, 1993. A simple introduction to rocks and minerals.

McDermott, Gerald. *Coyote: A Trickster Tale from the American Southwest.* Harcourt, 1994. Coyote tries to fly.

Oughton, Jerrie. *The Magic Weaver of Rugs.* Houghton Mifflin, 1994. Spider Woman teaches two Navajo women to weave.

Parker, Steve. *Rocks and Minerals.* DK Publishing, 1993. A brief introduction to rocks and minerals including activities.

Posell, Elsa. *Deserts.* Children's Press, 1982. Describes deserts and some of the animals, plants and people that live in them.

Roessel, Monty. *Songs from the Loom: A Navajo Girl Learns to Weave.* Lerner Publishing Group, 1995. A look at the process of weaving Navajo rugs and its importance to Navajo culture.

Coyote Puppet Hat Pattern

Materials:

- crayons
- scissors
- paste, tape or stapler
- construction paper

Instructions:

1. Copy the coyote.

2. Color it, then cut out.

3. Cut a band from construction paper approximately 1" wide and long enough make a headband. Tape or staple together.

4. Staple or tape the coyote to the front.

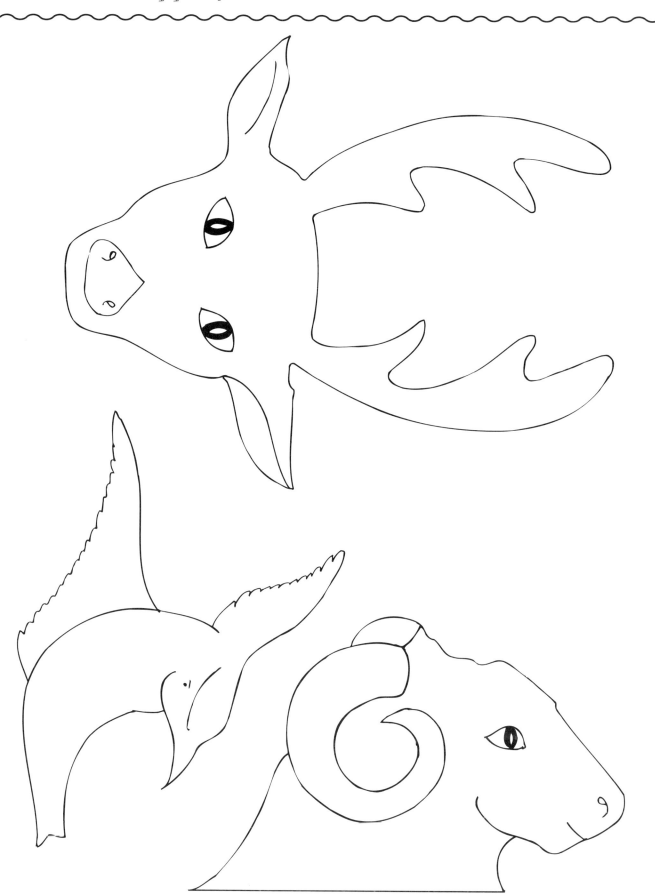

Finger Puppet Patterns

The Elves and the Shoemaker

Programming Ideas

Theme: Stores

Setting the Scene

Play a career guessing game by having the children try to finish the statement. For example: A tailor makes _____. A chef makes _____. A cobbler makes _____. Explain that the next story has a cobbler in it. What is another name for a cobbler? *(A shoemaker.)* Can anyone guess the name of the story?

Story

The Elves and the Shoemaker by Paul Galdone

Read the story. Ask the children to tell you anything they know about elves. (For example: Elves help Santa Claus.) Ask how people can learn more about elves. Model how to use a simple encyclopedia.

Puppets

Prepare two elf puppets (page 112–113) and create the shoemaker's shop in a section of the library or classroom (workbench, customer counter, etc.). Act out the story with two children using the elf puppets.

Activities

Careers/Bulletin Board

Discuss careers. Title a bulletin board "What I Might Be When I Grow Up." Make a graph of the choices and surround with magazine pictures and drawings of different careers. Ask the children to find out what jobs adults in their families have. Invite guest speakers. After this "career unit" make a new graph and compare any changes.

Consumer Skills

Design and decorate elf hats (page 112). Display the hats around the room. Have the children individually "buy" their hats back when you have some spare moments. For example: Give a child several play coins or overhead transparency coins. The child creates a combination, which adds up to 50 cents (or whatever price you designate). Review the combinations with the class. Read *The Elf's Hat, Hats, Hats, Hats* or *Caps for Sale.*

Mapmaking

Set up the shoemaker's shop in a section of the library or classroom. Show the children how to make a two-dimensional map of the shop or of the classroom on an overhead transparency. Have the children draw their own maps.

Math

Copy the elf hat (page 112) onto an overhead transparency. Write an operation sign (+, -, x, ÷) on the hat and numbers on either side. The student who answers correctly can come up and write a new equation for the class.

Social Studies

Discuss what the shoemaker and his wife might have done if the elves had not come to help or what they could do to keep business going well. One strategy could be advertising. Create some posters for the shoemaker's shop (or the hat shop if you did that activity). If a video camera is available, create a commercial or have a reporter conduct interviews. Have a shoe fashion show.

Books

Folktale Versions

Galdone, Paul. *The Elves and the Shoemaker.* Clarion Books, 1984. Elves help a poor shoemaker and his wife stay in business.

Littledale, Freya. *The Elves and the Shoemaker.* Scholastic, 1975. Two elves help a poor shoemaker and his wife stay in business.

Lowell, Susan. *The Bootmaker and the Elves.* Orchard Books, 1997. Elves help a poor bootmaker and his wife stay in business.

Watts, Bernadette. *The Elves and the Shoemaker.* North-South Books, 1986. Two tiny men help a poor shoemaker and his wife stay in business.

Related Reading

Morris, Ann. *Hats, Hats, Hats.* Lothrop, Lee & Shepard Books, 1989. A photographic look at hats around the world.

Slobodkina, Esphyr. *Caps for Sale.* HarperCollins, 1947. A cap peddler must outwit some mischievous monkeys.

Weninger, Brigitte. *The Elf's Hat.* North-South Books, 2000. An elf's hat makes a fine home for many animals until a flea joins the group.

Elf Puppet Instructions and Patterns

This puppet will work best if copied on heavier stock paper.

Materials:

- construction paper and/or heavier stock paper (white) if you are going to copy patterns to trace or color
- scissors
- straws (2 to 4 per puppet)
- paste
- tape
- brads
- crayons
- pencil
- ruler

Instructions:

1. Copy the elf patterns (enlarge to desired size).

2. Color the pieces or cut the pattern pieces out and trace around them on construction paper.

3. Cut out the pattern pieces.

4. Paste the head to the body.

5. Punch out all holes for the brads.

6. Assemble the arms behind the body and the legs behind the body.

7. Tape a ruler to the back center of the elf body.

8. Tape straws to the end of the hand. The feet are optional.

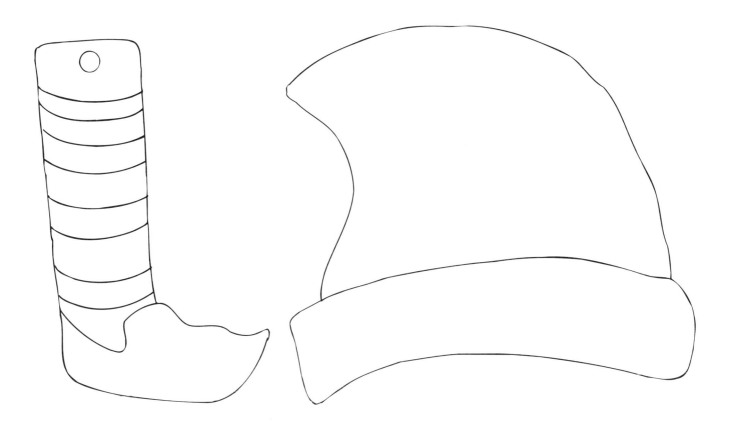

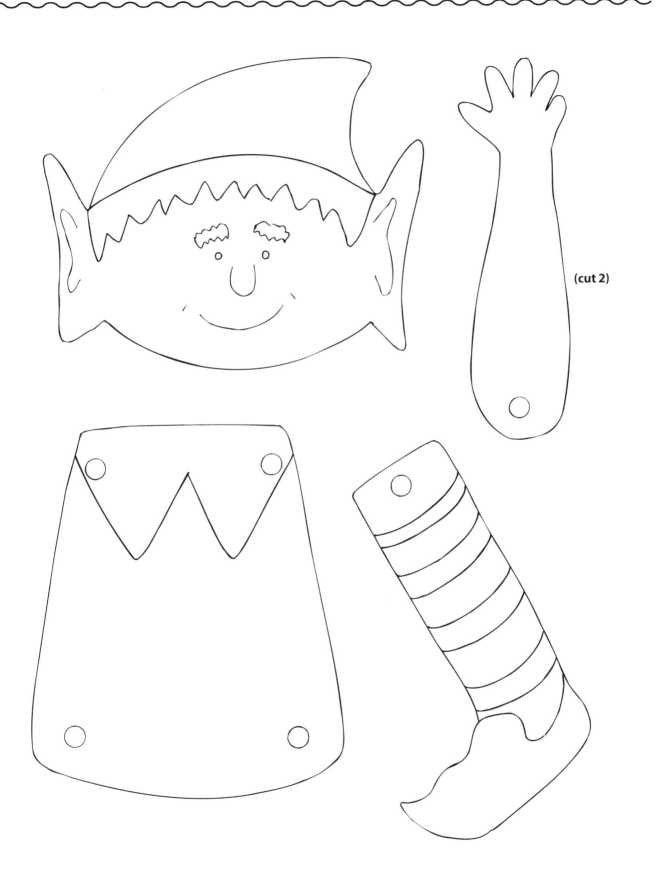

(cut 2)

The Funny Little Woman

Programming Ideas

Theme: Caves

Setting the Scene

Say: Are you afraid of the "wicked *oni*?" (oh-nee) No? Neither is the funny little woman! At the end of the story, we'll see if you know what an *oni* is. (An *oni* is a wicked monster in many Japanese stories.)

Story

The Funny Little Woman by Arlene Mosel

After reading the story, discuss caves. Ask: Was the funny little woman afraid in the cave? Should she have been? Why or why not? Read some of Silver's *Cave* aloud, then see if the answers change.

Puppet

After reading the story once, make *oni* puppets (page 116). Read the story again. The children can make the puppets say "Tee-he-he-he" whenever the phrase occurs in the story (even when it's the funny little woman's line).

Activities

Art

Draw caves or scenes from the story.

Cooking

Ask the children what they know about rice. Read *Rice Is Life* and then ask the children to list facts they learned from the book. Show them different kinds of rice and then make some. If possible, demonstrate how to use chopsticks.

Game—Statues

Play some music as the children move around to the beat. Stop the music. The children must freeze like a statue. Continue the stop/start pattern throughout the song.

Geography

Read parts of Silver's *Cave* or Siebert's *Cave*. Find books or magazine articles on famous caves. Then create a classroom bulletin board. Children can draw and cut out the animals they might find in a cave. Older children can create dioramas. Read books where caves are an important part of the story: *Ali Baba and the 40 Thieves, Beady Bear, Cave Boy, The Banza* or *Herbert the Timid Dragon.*

Math

Remind the students of how the rice doubled when it was stirred with the magic paddle. Demonstrate doubling by having the students stand up. Ask one to sit down. Prompt the children: 1 + 1 = ? How many children need to be sitting now? (Two.) Prompt: 2 + 2 = ?, etc. The whole class will probably be sitting in five to six steps. Read *The Rajah's Rice.*

Seasons

Look at the illustrations of the funny little woman's house. Discuss the passage of time and the change of seasons. Draw pictures of homes or of the school set in different seasons.

Books

Folktale Versions

Cole, Joanna (ed.). *Best-Loved Folktales of the World.* Doubleday, 1982. A collection of 200 folktales from around the world.

Mosel, Arlene. *The Funny Little Woman.* Dutton, 1972. A little woman pursues her dumpling and gets captured by oni monsters.

Related Reading

Barry, David. *The Rajah's Rice: A Mathematical Folktale From India.* W. H. Freeman and Company, 1994. A young girl saves the villagers from hunger with her knowledge of mathematics.

Dubowski, Cathy East, and Mark Dubowski. *Cave Boy.* Random House, 1988. A cave boy likes to invent things.

Freeman, Don. *Beady Bear.* Puffin, 1954. A toy bear tries living in a cave.

Gelman, Rita Golden. *Rice Is Life.* Henry Holt & Company, 2000. Shows the importance of rice to the Balinese people.

José, Eduard. *Ali Baba and the 40 Thieves.* Child's World, 1988. A man discovers the treasure thieves have hidden in a cave.

Mayer, Mercer. *Herbert the Timid Dragon.* Golden Books, 1991. A dragon leaves his cave to become a knight.

Siebert, Diane. *Cave.* HarperCollins, 2000. A poetic look at caves and their inhabitants.

Silver, Donald M. *Cave.* W. H. Freeman and Company, 1993. An overview of caves and their inhabitants, plus activities.

Wolkstein, Diane. *The Banza: A Haitian Story.* Puffin, 1984. A goat receives a gift from the tiger that became her friend.

Oni Puppet Instructions

Materials:

- construction paper
- scissors
- pencil
- crayons or markers
- lunch bags
- paste

Directions:

1. Copy the pattern on heavier stock paper for tracing, or copy the pattern for students to color.

2. Trace the pieces and cut them out. Make sure the large beard is on the fold.

3. Paste the large beard to the bag bottom.

4. Paste the horns, teeth and eyes onto the oni face.

5. Paste the head over the beard.

6. Paste the side beards on the face.

3

5

6

Oni Puppet Patterns

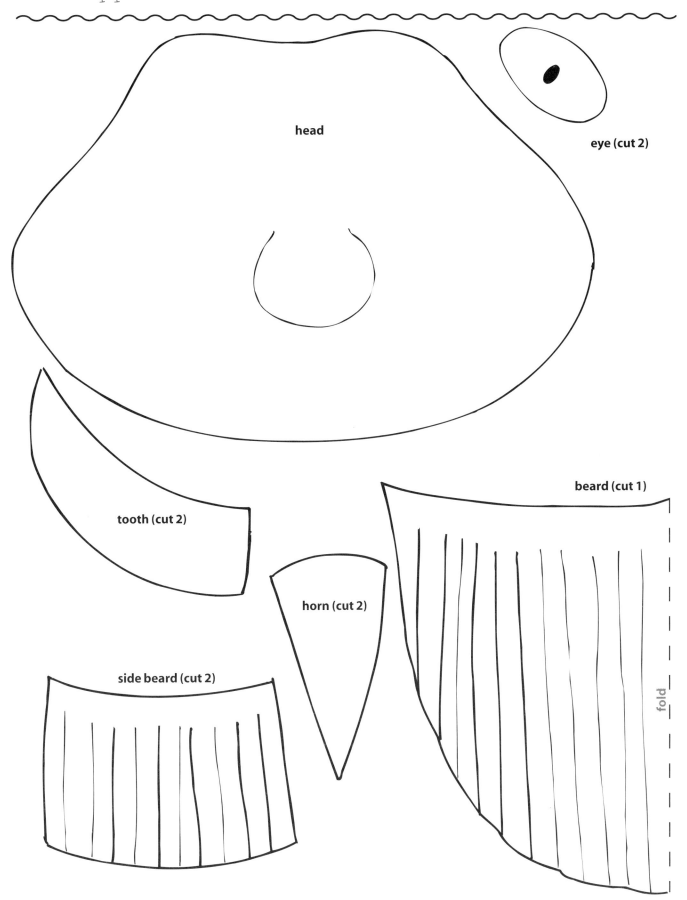

head

eye (cut 2)

tooth (cut 2)

beard (cut 1)

horn (cut 2)

side beard (cut 2)

fold

The Gingerbread Man

Programming Ideas

Theme: Neighborhoods

Setting the Scene

Ask the students to think about their neighborhoods. Ask: If you left your house or your apartment, who are some of the people you would see? Would you see any animals? In the story you are about to read, the main character sees an old woman, an old man, a pig, a dog, a horse, a cow and finally a fox when he leaves the house. Can anyone guess the story? (If they need another hint: "I'll run and run as fast as I can. You can't catch me. I'm the _____.")

Story

The Gingerbread Man by Eric A. Kimmel

Read the story once. Ask if anyone has the gingerbread man's speech memorized. Review it. Read the story again and have the children say the speech with you when it occurs.

Puppets

Prepare a large puppet of the Gingerbread Man (page 120) and enlarge the pictures of the old woman, old man, the pig, the dog, the cow, the horse and the fox (page 121). Act out the story by having different children hold or wear the pictures and stand throughout the classroom. As you read the story, a student using the Gingerbread Man puppet goes to the students with the appropriate pictures and acts out the story as you read.

Activities

Cooking

Make gingerbread people. While they are baking, search for the gingerbread man around the school (based on clues written and placed previously). For example: I have gone to read a book. Do you know where you should look? (Media center.) I like to sing, don't you? Can you find me with this clue? (Music room.)

Game

In many stories foxes are tricky and smart. Read *Flossie and the Fox* for a story where a girl outsmarts the fox. Then play a guessing game where students try to guess the animal. For example: The leader might say, "I have sharp claws and yellow eyes. What am I?" The person who guesses the animal gets to become the leader. If no one has the correct answer after three guesses, the leader gives another clue. After three clues, if there is no correct answer, the leader tells the animal and picks the next leader.

Literature

According to *The Arbuthnot Anthology of Children's Literature*, the story of the Gingerbread Man is an American version of an older folktale, possibly "The Wee Bannock" (Scotland), "The Pancake" (Scandinavia) or "The Johnny Cake" (England). Whatever its origin, "The Gingerbread Man" is a cumulative tale because of its repetitious but expanding refrain. Read other cumulative stories like *The Old Woman and Her Pig, Ask Mr. Bear, Too Much Noise* or *The Little Old Lady Who Was Not Afraid of Anything.*

Mapmaking

As a class, draw a map of what the Gingerbread Man's neighborhood might look like. Have the children make simple maps of their neighborhoods. (Refer to *Mapmaking with Children* for more in-depth mapping activities.)

Movement and Math

Ask the children how long it would take the Gingerbread Man to run across the room (or another given distance). Using a stopwatch, time how long it takes student volunteers to run that distance. Chart the times by making a bar graph on the board or by copying several clock patterns (page 122) onto an overhead transparency and coloring in the number of seconds each student raced onto clocks. Teach the student to look at the second hand of a clock and time each other.

Storytelling

Review the characters the gingerbread man met in his neighborhood. Read Egielski's *The Gingerbread Boy*. Review the characters met in that neighborhood. Brainstorm the characters the gingerbread man might meet if he ran from the classroom. Tell the story. Challenge the children to make up a story for their own neighborhoods if the gingerbread man ran from their houses or apartments.

Books

Folktale Versions

Arbuthnot, May Hill (ed.). *The Arbuthnot Anthology of Children's Literature.* Scott, Foresman and Company, 1953. A collection of poems and stories for children including "The Gingerbread Boy."

Brett, Jan. *Gingerbread Baby.* Putnam, 1999. A gingerbread baby escapes from the oven and runs through the countryside receiving unexpected aid.

Egielski, Richard. *The Gingerbread Boy.* Laura Geringer Books, 1997. The gingerbread boy escapes from the oven and runs through a city.

Kimmel, Eric A. *The Gingerbread Man.* Holiday House, 1993. A gingerbread man escapes from the oven and runs through the countryside.

Related Reading

Flack, Marjorie. *Ask Mr. Bear.* Aladdin Books, 1932. A young boy asks some animals what he should get his mother for her birthday.

Kimmel, Eric A. *The Old Woman and Her Pig.* Holiday House, 1992. An old woman recruits the help of many others to get her pig over a stile.

McGovern, Ann. *Too Much Noise.* Houghton Mifflin, 1967. A tale of a man who asks a wise man for advice to help him with his noisy home.

McKissack, Patricia C. *Flossie and the Fox.* Dial, 1986. A little girl insists that a fox prove he is a fox before she will be frightened.

Sobel, David. *Mapmaking with Children: Sense-of-Place Education for the Elementary Years.* Heinemann, 1998. Theory and activities for developing mapmaking skills in the elementary child.

Williams, Linda. *The Little Old Lady Who Was Not Afraid of Anything.* Harper & Row, 1986. A little old lady is almost frightened on her walk home.

Gingerbread Man Puppet Directions

Materials:

- paper
- popsicle sticks
- scissors
- crayons or markers
- paste or tape

Directions:

1. Photocopy the pattern on page 120.
2. Color the gingerbread men and cut around the rectangle.
3. Fold the pattern in half at the dotted line.
4. Attach the stick to the inside.
5. Tape or paste closed.

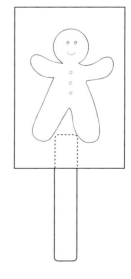

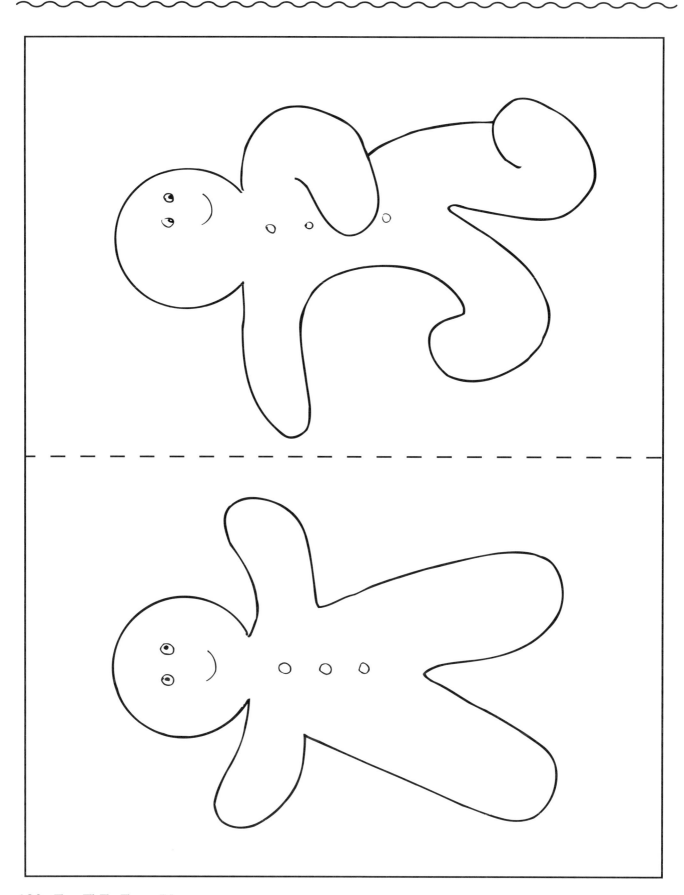

The Gingerbread Man Additional Characters

Materials:

- card stock or paper
- yarn
- scissors
- crayons or markers
- paste
- hole punch

Directions:

1. Enlarge the pictures.

2. Color and cut them out.

3. Punch two holes on the top of each picture.

4. Cut yarn to the desired length and run it through the holes.

5. Knot the ends of the yarn and hang the pictures over the children's heads.

Tip: Laminate or mount the pictures on construction paper if using regular paper.

Clock Pattern

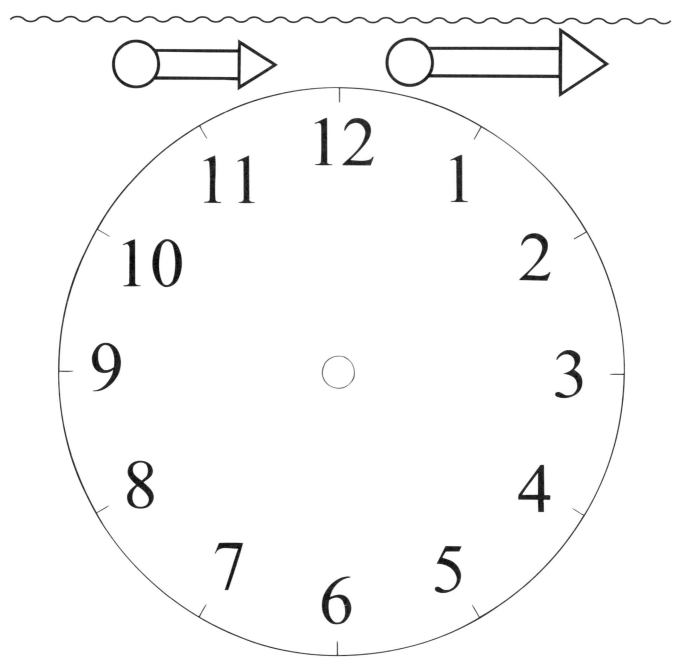

Materials:

- poster board
- paste
- hole punch
- brads (1 per clock)

Directions:

1. Copy the clock pattern and paste it on a piece of poster board.

2. Cut the clock hands patterns from different colors of construction paper.

3. Punch a hole in each hand and in the center of the clock.

4. Place the small hand on top of the large hand, matching the holes.

5. Run the brad through the hands and the clock.

6. Bend the brad in the back.

How Ma-Ui Fished Up the Great Island

Programming Ideas

Theme: Oceans and Islands

Setting the Scene

Ask the children if anyone has ever hurt their feelings. Explain that the story you are about to read has a boy in it whose brothers called him lazy because he didn't catch fish as well as they. He had even invented things they had used and they still called him lazy. The boy's name is Maui. Can you guess what he caught one day when fishing with his brothers? Let's read and find out.

Story

How Ma-Ui Fished Up the Great Island
by Joanna Cole

Enlarge and copy coloring pictures (page 126). Explain that you are going to read a story that has no pictures. The children are to color the picture and listen. If they finish coloring before the story is finished, they can color another ocean scene on the back. After reading, ask the children if they can name the island that Ma-Ui fished up. *(Hawaii.)* Locate Hawaii on a map and then read *Hawaii Is a Rainbow*.

Puppets

Make the Ma-Ui puppet (page 125) on card stock and attach to a ruler or paint stick. Have the children make up a new story for Ma-Ui, creating any props needed (such as what he might fish up next). Split into pairs to tell each other's stories. Read other Maui stories such as *How Maui Slowed the Sun*.

Activities

Art

Read *Under the Water, What Do You See Under the Sea?* or look through *Ocean Animals*. Draw underwater creatures and plants with wax crayons, but leave the background blank. Paint over with dark blue paint, which will cover the background but not the wax.

Geography

Oceans. Ask: What is an ocean? Read *The Earth Is Mostly Ocean* or *Oceans*. Explain that "How Ma-Ui Fished Up the Great Island" took place in the Pacific Ocean. Locate the Pacific Ocean and Hawaii on a globe. Compare it to where you are now.

Islands. Explain that there are four kinds of islands: continental, oceanic (volcanic), coral and barrier. Hawaii is an oceanic island. Make a volcano model. (Directions can be found in many science project books.) Read stories set on islands such as *The Little Island, The Disappearing Island, Lost In the Storm* or *Tom Foolery*. Try to figure out what kinds of islands are featured in the stories.

Hawaiian Luau Day

Have a special Hawaiian luau day where the children wear grass skirts, make leis, dance the hula, eat fruit at a luau, learn some of the language and play games.

Science

Test the buoyancy of different objects. Read *Curious George Rides a Bike* and make paper boats.

Books

Folktale Versions

Cole, Joanna (ed.). *Best-Loved Folktales of the World.* Doubleday, 1982. A collection of 200 folktales from around the world.

Williams, Julie Stewart. *Maui Goes Fishing.* Kolowalu, 1991. Maui pulls up the islands of Hawaii with a magic fish hook.

Related Reading

Broekel, Ray. *Experiments With Water.* Children's Press, 1988. Simple experiments that demonstrate properties of water.

Carrick, Carol. *Lost In the Storm.* Clarion Books, 1974. Two boys worry about a dog lost in a storm overnight.

Carter, Katharine Jones. *Oceans.* Children's Press, 1982. An introduction to oceans.

Chinery, Michael. *Ocean Animals.* Random House, 1991. An introduction to ocean animals from albatrosses to whales.

Demas, Corinne. *The Disappearing Island.* Simon & Schuster, 2000. A grandmother and granddaughter visit an island at low tide.

Feeney, Stephanie. *Hawaii Is a Rainbow.* Kolowalu Books, 1985. A photographic tour of Hawaii highlighting colors.

Fowler, Allan. *The Earth Is Mostly Ocean.* Children's Press, 1995. An introduction to the ocean.

Kalman, Bobbie. *What Do You See Under the Sea?* Crabtree, 1995. Photographs of people and creatures underwater near a coral reef.

MacDonald, Golden. *The Little Island.* Yearling, 1993. A little kitten learns the little island's secret.

Parkinson, Curtis. *Tom Foolery.* Bradbury Press, 1993. A cat falls off his boat and has an island adventure.

Rey, H. A. *Curious George Rides a Bike.* Houghton Mifflin, 1952. Curious George has several adventures when he gets a new bike.

Tune, Suelyn Ching. *How Maui Slowed the Sun.* Kolowalu Books, 1988. Maui slows the sun using his magical powers.

Ziefert, Harriet. *Under the Water.* Puffin Books, 1990. A snorkler looks at plants and animals under the water.

Ma-Ui Puppet Pattern

Materials:

- card stock
- crayons or markers
- rulers or paint sticks
- scissors
- tape

Directions:

1. Photocopy the puppet.

2. Color the puppet and cut it out.

3. Attach it to a paint stick or ruler with tape.

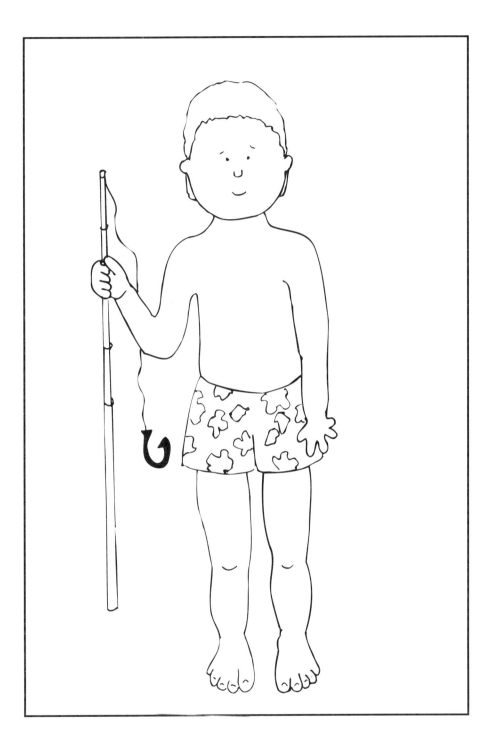

It Could Always Be Worse

Programming Ideas

Theme: Houses and Homes

Setting the Scene

Put a rug at the front of the room. Ask the children to pretend that it is a one-room house. Have one child stand on the rug. Ask: Do you have room to move around? (Yes.) Add another child and ask the question again. Continue until the rug is crowded.

Story

It Could Always Be Worse by Margot Zemach

Explain that the story is about a large family with six children who live in a one-room house. It gets so crowded and noisy that the father goes to a wise man, the village rabbi, for advice on what to do. Read the story.

Puppets

Make finger puppets (page 129) and copy the house picture (page 130) for each student. The students will prop up the house picture on their desks. They can either tape their house to an open book or use a strip of folded poster board to make the house stand up. The rabbi is a stand-alone puppet while the others can be taped to the fingers. Read the story again while the children act out the story with the puppets.

Activities

Creative Writing

Discuss what you would need if the class had to live in the classroom. Create your own classroom story where the teacher runs to the principal for advice. The principal can advise them to bring in anything—pets, dinosaurs, a circus, whatever! Students can simply enjoy the storytelling process or illustrate a classroom book.

Literature

Ask the children if they know what a folktale is. Explain that a folktale is a story that people told from generation to generation before it became common to write stories down. Explain that many different people can retell folktales. Read other versions of the story such as *Too Much Noise, A Big Quiet House* or the version in the Cole collection.

Mapmaking

Read *Houses and Homes* and discuss homes around the world. Ask the children to draw a simple map of their own homes with at least one thing about the house, apartment or yard they can share with the class. (Refer to *Mapmaking with Children* for more in-depth mapping activities.)

Music and Movement

Ask the children to clap their hands however they want to. Ask if that was noisy. Now have the children all clap a steady beat at the same time following your example. Ask if that was noisy. Explain that one thing that separates music from noise is rhythm. Teach some hand clapping games from *Hand Clap!* or make up your own.

Science

One sentence from the story stated "in winter, when the nights were long and the days were cold, life was especially hard." Find your location on the globe and mark it somehow. Then ask a student to be the sun. Demonstrate how the earth tilts during its revolution. Read a book featuring a wintry setting (e.g., *Winter*) and discuss the winter season.

Books

Folktale Versions

Cole, Joanna (ed.). *Best-Loved Folktales of the World.* Doubleday, 1982. A collection of 200 folktales from around the world.

Forest, Heather. *A Big Quiet House: A Yiddish Folktale from Eastern Europe.* August House, 1996. A Yiddish tale of a man who asks a wise woman for advice to help him with his crowded and noisy home.

McGovern, Ann. *Too Much Noise.* Houghton Mifflin, 1967. A tale of a man who asks a wise man for advice to help him with his noisy home.

Zemach, Margot. *It Could Always Be Worse.* Farrar, Straus and Giroux. 1976. A Yiddish tale of a man who asks his rabbi for advice to help him with his crowded and noisy home.

Related Reading

Bernstein, Sara. *Hand Clap! "Miss Mary Mack" and 42 Other Hand-Clapping Games for Kids.* Adams Media, 1994. Words and directions are provided for 43 hand-clapping games.

Hirschi, Ron. *Winter.* Cobblehill Books, 1990. Photographs and text depict wintry nature scenes.

Leodhas, Sorche Nic. *Always Room for One More.* Holt, Rinehart and Winston, 1965. A Scottish family welcomes all into their home and their kindness is repaid.

Morris, Ann. *Houses and Homes.* Lothrop, Lee & Shepard Books, 1992. A photographic look at houses around the world.

Sobel, David. *Mapmaking with Children: Sense-of-Place Education for the Elementary Years.* Heinemann, 1998. Theory and activities for developing mapmaking skills in the elementary child.

Rabbi Stand-alone Puppet

It Could Always Be Worse Finger Puppets

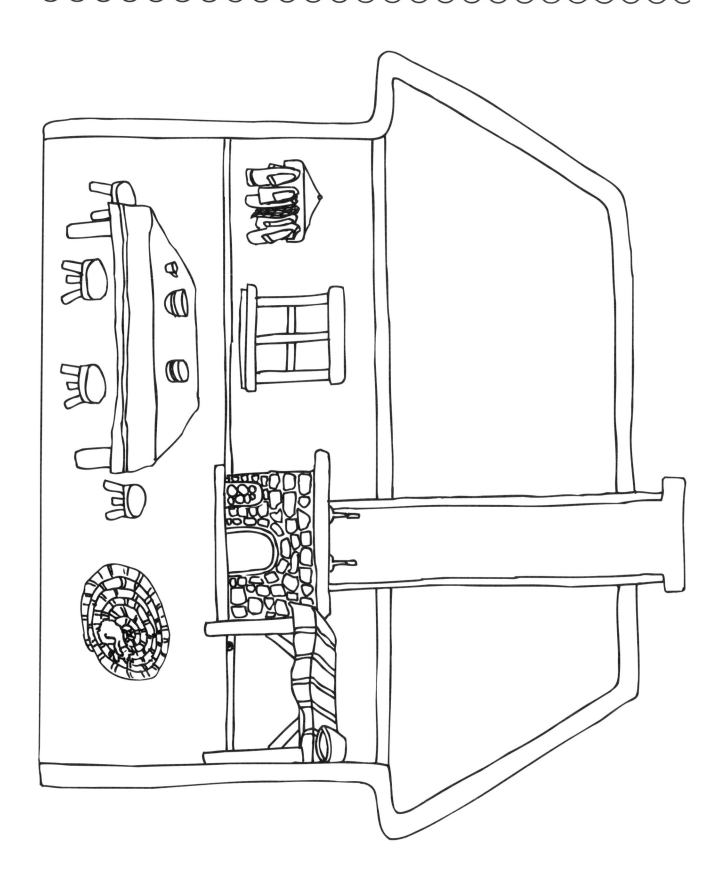

Momotaro (The Peach Boy)

Programming Ideas

Theme: Rivers

Setting the Scene

Ask the children to picture in their minds an old woman washing her clothes on a rock in a river. "Squish, squish, squish. With every squish the old woman said, 'I wish, I wish, I wish.'" What do you think she wished for? Can you guess what she got? (A huge peach ... that had a baby boy inside!)

Story

Peach Boy by William H. Hooks

Explain that rivers are important in a lot of stories, perhaps because they are important to people. Among other things, they provide fresh water, transportation, fish, energy and fun. Towns and cities are often built near rivers. The characters in the story you are about to hear live near a river in Japan. Locate Japan on a map and read the story.

Puppets

After reading the story, make puppets (page 133). Practice telling the story or make up new quests for the characters to take.

Activities

Art

Read other versions of the story, *The Funny Little Woman, Where the Wild Things Are* or other stories with *onis* (monsters in Japanese folklore), ogres or monsters. Compare the illustrations in the stories. Draw monsters and share.

Community Service

Build a fort with canned goods. Read *Peach Boy* again and discuss sharing. Donate the goods to a worthy charity.

Geography

Copy a world map onto an overhead transparency. Using a thin blue pen, trace over some of the major rivers such as the Amazon, the Ganges, the Mississippi and the Nile. Read *Rivers* or *All Along the River.* Discuss. Challenge the children to look at a globe to see if they can find any rivers.

Graphing

Bring in some peaches, apples and oranges. Before sampling the fruit, survey the children to see which fruit is preferred. Graph the result. Try the fruit and see if the answers (and thus the graph) have changed.

Science

Read *The Water Cycle* or *The Magic School Bus Wet All Over* and discuss. Try creating your own water cycle model. Books such as *Living Geography* provide directions.

Storytelling

Momotaro goes on a journey and is joined by three companions: a dog, a monkey and a hawk. If you were on a journey, what three animals would you like to meet? Draw a picture of the four of you and tell a friend a story based on the picture.

Treasure Hunt

Make a treasure map where the children must follow a route and end at a treasure. Pack a snack like Momotaro did and enjoy a treat when you get to the goal.

Books

Folktale Versions

Cole, Joanna (ed.). *Best-Loved Folktales of the World.* Doubleday, 1982. A collection of 200 folktales from around the world.

Hooks, William H. *Peach Boy.* Byron Press, 1992. An elderly couple is blessed with a son who rescues their village from monsters with the help of some animals.

McCarthy, Ralph F. *The Adventures of Momotaro, the Peach Boy.* Kodansha International, 1993. An elderly couple is blessed with a son who rescues their village from monsters with the help of some animals.

Sakurai, Gail. *Peach Boy: A Japanese Legend.* Troll, 1993. An elderly couple is blessed with a son who rescues their village from monsters with the help of some animals.

Related Reading

Fowler, Allan. *All Along the River.* Children's Press, 1994. An overview of rivers.

Frost, Helen. *The Water Cycle.* Pebble Books, 2000. A simple description of the water cycle with photographs.

Mosel, Arlene. *The Funny Little Woman.* Dutton, 1972. A little woman pursues her dumpling and gets captured by oni monsters.

Owen, Andy, and Miranda Ashwell. *Rivers.* Heinemann, 1998. An overview of rivers with some aerial photos and examples of maps.

Relf, Patricia, Brachen, Carolyn, and Cole, Joanna. *The Magic School Bus Wet All Over: A Book About the Water Cycle.* Scholastic, 1996. Ms. Frizzle and her class become part of the water cycle.

Sendak, Maurice. *Where the Wild Things Are.* HarperCollins, 1988. A young boy has a wild adventure after he is sent to his room without his supper.

Taylor, Barbara. *Living Geography.* Two-Can Publishing, 2001. Weather, ocean, river and map experiments and activities.

Momotaro Puppet Instructions

Materials:

- construction paper
  (black, beige or pink, other colors)
- scissors
- paste
- markers or crayons
- pencil
- paper lunch bags

Directions:

1. Enlarge patterns (pages 134–135) to 105%. Trace and cut out the pattern pieces from construction paper.

2. Paste the hair on the face.

3. Paste the headband in the head.

4. Paste the head on the bottom of the bag.

5. Lift the bottom and paste on the kimono.

6. Paste the hands on the kimono.

7. Use markers or crayons for details.

Momotaro Puppet Patterns

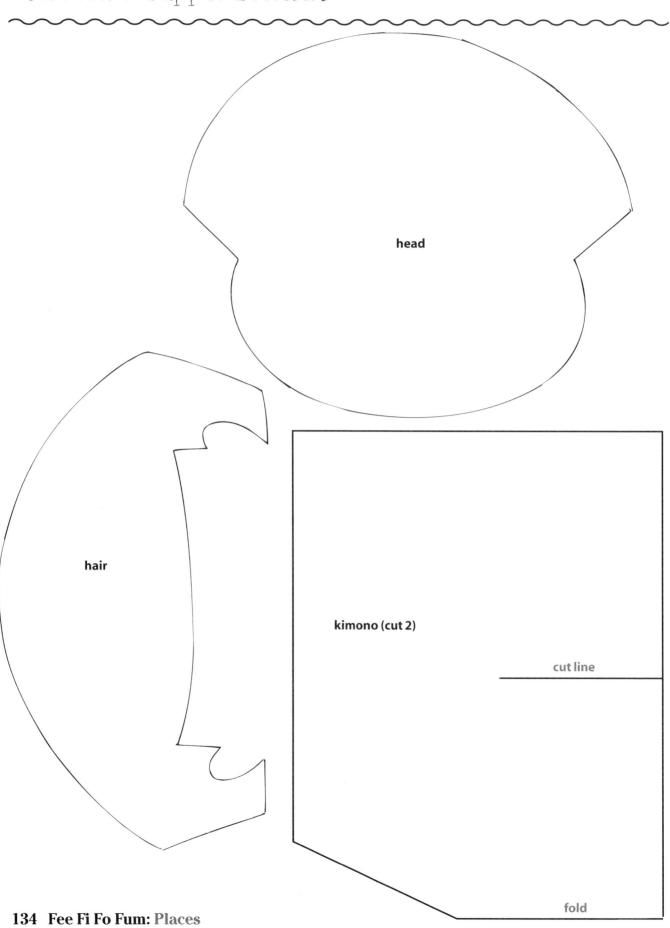

head

hair

kimono (cut 2)

cut line

fold

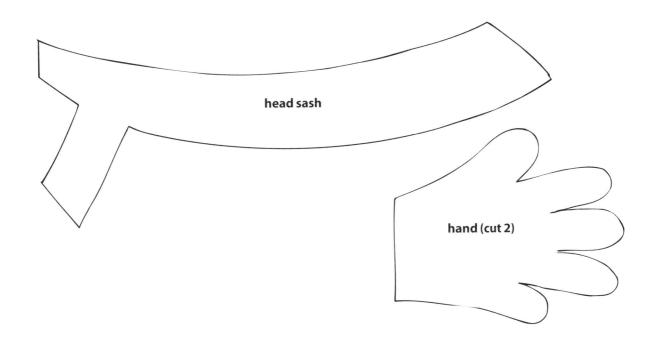

head sash

hand (cut 2)

Finger Puppet Patterns

Materials:

- scissors
- crayons or markers
- tape

Directions:

1. Photocopy the puppets. You might want to make a master of multiple puppets on a page.

2. Color the puppets and cut them out.

3. Roll a piece of tape and place it on the back of the puppet. Attach the puppet to your finger.

Three Billy Goats Gruff

Programming Ideas

Theme: Hills and Mountains

Setting the Scene

Ask: Has anyone ever heard the expression "the grass is always greener on the other side of the fence?" Explain that the story you are about to read has grass that is greener on the other side of the river. The three main characters want to cross that river to get to "a distant hillside where the grass was especially tall and green and tender." Can anyone name the story?

Story

The Three Billy Goats Gruff by Glen Rounds

Explain that the story is from a country called Norway. Identify the country on a map. Explain that Norway has a lot of hills and mountains. Read the story.

Puppets

Make the four popsicle stick puppets (page 138). If possible, make a backdrop for the story on a bulletin board using construction paper or kraft paper that shows two hills and the bridge. After making the puppets, tell the story to the class, using the puppets in front of the bulletin board. Ask for volunteers to come up to tell the story using the puppets. Challenge the children to do a puppet show at home for their families. **Note:** The bulletin board can then be titled "Bridge to Reading." Put commonly paired words, such as peanut butter "and" jelly, on either side of a bridge. Write the word "and" over the bridge. Practice reading and matching.

Activities

Animals

Read *Goats* and *Mountain Goats.* Use a Venn diagram to compare and contrast the two. (For example: a mountain goat is not a goat!) Encourage the children to make up puppet stories that use some of the information.

Folklore

There are hills and mountains on every continent, and many folktales, like *Three Billy Goats Gruff,* use them as settings. Read *Tikki Tikki Tembo, Borreguita and the Coyote, The Legend of the Indian Paintbrush, The Crystal Mountain* or *Nine-In-One Grr! Grr!* Look at how the mountains are illustrated. Draw an illustration to go with one of the stories.

Geography

Ask the children to explain what hills and mountains are. Do they know the difference between the two? *(Mountains are taller, sharper and steeper whereas hills are under 2,000 feet and more rounded.)* Tell the children that you are going to read a nonfiction book (such as *The Mountains*). It has a lot of facts in it. Ask each student to remember one fact they find particularly interesting to share with the class when the book is finished. Share facts. Go through the book again and discuss some of the pages.

Music

Read *Bill Grogan's Goat*, then learn the song.

Science

Ask the class why grass is green. Try an experiment to see if sunlight is needed. Put a brick or board over a grassy area. Check daily to see if the grass changes colors. (It will turn yellow.) Then remove the brick or board to discover if the grass will turn green again.

Books

Folktale Versions

Cole, Joanna (ed.). *Best-Loved Folktales of the World.* Doubleday, 1982. A collection of 200 folktales from around the world.

McKissack, Patricia, and Fredrick McKissack. *Three Billy Goats Gruff.* Children's Press, 1987. Three clever goats outwit a troll.

Rounds, Glen. *Three Billy Goats Gruff.* Holiday House, 1993. Three clever goats outwit a troll.

Stevens, Janet. *The Three Billy Goats Gruff.* Harcourt, 1987. Three clever goats outwit a troll.

Related Reading

Aardema, Verna. *Borreguita and the Coyote.* Knopf, 1991. A little lamb outwits a coyote.

De Paola, Tomie. *The Legend of the Indian Paintbrush.* Putnam, 1988. A young man is true to his artistic gifts and is able to bring the colors of the sunset down to the earth.

Hansen, Ann Larkin. *Goats.* ABDO Publishing, 1998. An overview of domesticated goats.

Higginson, Mel. *The Mountains.* Rourke Corporation, 1994. Describes mountains and life that survives there.

Hoberman, Mary Ann. *Bill Grogan's Goat.* Megan Tingley Books, 2002. A goat eats three red shirts and gets in trouble.

Ivy, Bill. *Mountain Goats.* Grolier, 1986. An overview of mountain goats.

Mosel, Arlene. *Tikki Tikki Tembo.* Scholastic, 1968. Tikki Tikki Tembo almost drowns in a well because of his great long name.

Sanderson, Ruth. *The Crystal Mountain.* Little, Brown and Company, 1999. Three sons search for their mother's tapestry.

Xiong, Blia, and adapted by Cathy Spagnoli. *Nine-In-One Grr! Grr!* Children's Book Press, 1989. Bird prevents the land from becoming overrun by tigers with quick thinking.

Three Billy Goats Gruff Puppet Directions

Materials:

- card stock or paper
- popsicle sticks or pencils
- scissors
- crayons or markers
- tape or paste

Directions:

1. Photocopy the puppets (page 138).

2. Color the puppets and cut them out.

3. Attach a stick or pencil to the back of each puppet.

Three Billy Goats Gruff Puppet Patterns

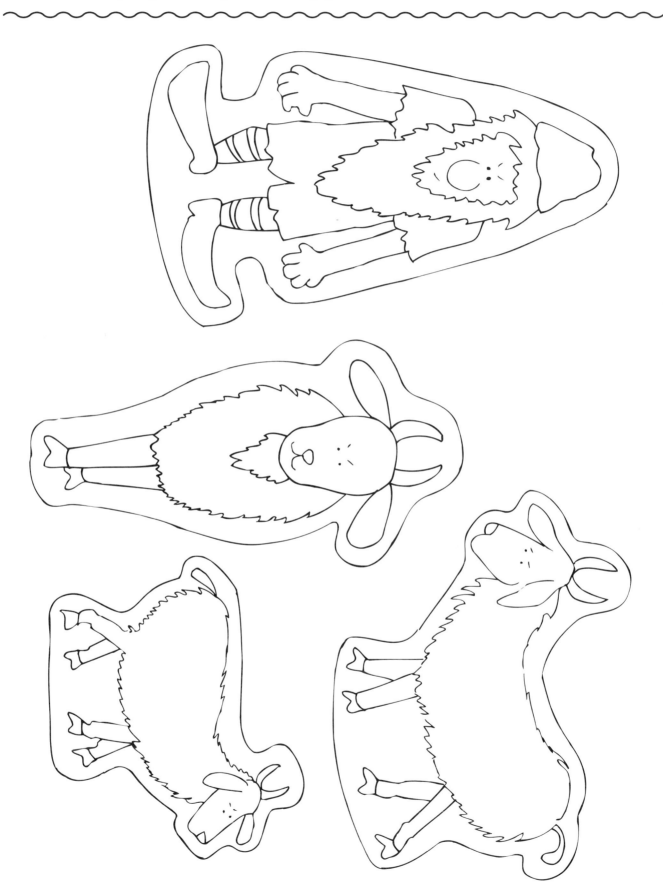

Wiley and the Hairy Man

Programming Ideas

Theme: Swamps and Wetlands

Setting the Scene

Write the words desert, forest, ocean and swamp on the board. Post pictures if possible. Ask the children where they would find the following creatures or plants: alligators, wild pigs, bamboo, opossums, mosquitoes, etc. (**Note:** Some may be in more than one place, but all should be in the swamp category.) Explain that the story you are about to read takes place in a swamp.

Story

Wiley and the Hairy Man by Molly Garrett Bang

Prepare the sequence cards (page 142). Read the story and then try to put the sequence cards in order. Ask a student to explain the part of the story shown on the first card, etc. Read the story again to see if they remembered the story right.

Puppets

Make Hairy Man bag puppets (page 141) and popsicle sticks for the other characters. Retell the story or make up new stories.

Activities

Creative Writing

Ask the children what animal they would like to be if they could change shapes like the Hairy Man did. Write a story about what happens if they were to change into that animal for a day. Younger children can draw a picture of the animal and tell why they would want to be that animal.

Geography

As a class, brainstorm any words and facts that come to mind when you say "swamp." Read a nonfiction book such as *Wild and Swampy*, *Wetlands* or *Life In*

A Wetland and story books such as *Over the Steamy Swamp, Liza Lou and the Yeller Belly Swamp, Petite Rouge* or *The Wide-Mouthed Frog.* Again brainstorm any words and facts that come to mind when you say "swamp." If possible, compare the two sessions, elaborate and correct any mistakes. Discuss the term "wetlands."

Magic Show

Discuss the conjuring and magic in the book. Teach the children some simple magic tricks. Have a magic show. Make a master of ceremonies puppet (page 143) to introduce the acts.

Music

Read *Mama Don't Allow* and learn the song. Tell the class they are a "swamp band" and play rhythm instruments as they sing the song or play along to zydeco recordings.

Poetry/Bulletin Board

As a class, write an acrostic poem for Wiley. *Poetry from A to Z* has some good tips. As a class or individually as homework, make poems for all of the children in the class. Decorate the poems and post them on a bulletin board entitled "What's in a Name?" Look up the meanings to the more common names in a book or on the Internet.

For example:

W   ise

I   s Wiley because he

L   istens to his mother

E   ven when he's scared.

Y   ahoo! The Hairy Man is gone for good!

Safety

Ask: Was the Hairy Man dangerous? How did Wiley stay safe? Read *Dinosaurs, Beware!* and discuss ways to stay safe.

Books

Folktale Versions

Bang, Molly Garrett. *Wiley and the Hairy Man.* Aladdin Books, 1976. A boy and his mother outwit the Hairy Man.

Sierra, Judy. *Wiley and the Hairy Man.* Lodestar Books, 1996. A boy and his mother outwit the Hairy Man.

Related Reading

Arnosky, Jim. *Wild And Swampy: Exploring with Jim Arnosky.* HarperCollins, 2000. A travel journal exploration of a swamp.

Artell, Mike. *Petite Rouge: A Cajun Red Riding Hood.* Dial, 2001. A young duck outwits a crocodile with the help of a cat.

Brown, Marc, and Stephen Krensky. *Dinosaurs, Beware! A Safety Guide.* Little, Brown and Company, 1982. Dinosaurs demonstrate safety at home, in the yard, with animals, etc.

Fowler, Allan. *Life In a Wetland.* Children's Press, 1998. An overview of wetlands including swamps, marshes and bogs.

Geraghty, Paul. *Over the Steamy Swamp.* Voyager Books, 1988. A mosquito starts a food chain reaction.

Hurd, Thacher. *Mama Don't Allow.* Harper & Row, 1984. Miles and his friends start a band and play for the Alligator Ball.

Janeczko, Paul B. (ed.). *Poetry from A to Z: A Guide for Young Writers.* Bradbury Press, 1994. Provides poems and directions for writing different kinds of poetry.

Leyton, Lawrence. *My First Magic Book.* DK Publishing. 1993. Gives directions for making magic props and using them.

Mayer, Mercer. *Liza Lou and the Yeller Belly Swamp.* Aladdin, 1976. Liza Lou outwits some nasty inhabitants of the Yeller Belly Swamp.

Schneider, Rex. *The Wide-Mouthed Frog.* Stemmer House, 1980. A frog asks other animals what he should eat instead of flies and mosquitoes.

Stoddard, Edward. *The First Book of Magic.* Avon Books, 1980. Directions for tricks with handkerchiefs, string, money, balls, cards, paper, etc.

Stone, Lynn M. *Wetlands.* Rourke Corporation, 1996. An overview of wetlands including swamps, marshes and bogs.

Wiley and the Hairy Man Puppet Instructions

Materials:

- paper bags (lunch size)
- construction paper (brown or black)
- scissors
- black markers or crayons
- glue or stapler
- pencil
- ruler

Directions:

1. Fold the construction paper in half. With fold at the top, draw lines as shown below.

2. Cut on the lines, making sure not to cut to the very top.

3. Cut a beard shape at the bottom and top. You will have two beards.

4. Glue or staple one to the bag, then the other over the top to form a beard.

5. Use a smaller sheet of construction paper for the hair and follow the same process you did for the beard.

6. Draw the hairy man's nose and eyes.

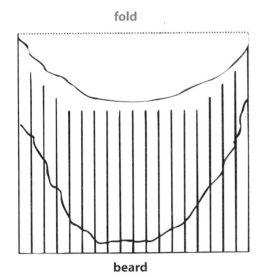

beard

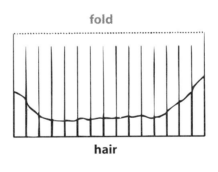

hair

Wiley and the Hairy Man Sequence Cards

Materials:

- scissors
- crayons or markers
- paste or tape
- poster board

Directions:

1. Photocopy the pictures, enlarging if desired.

2. Color the pictures and cut them out.

3. Mount each picture on a piece of slightly larger poster board.